The Vision of Fred
Friend of Poets—
Ami des Poètes

We would like to acknowledge the invaluable contribution of Wendy Scott, Fred's official biographer, in the final compilation and confirmation of the Selected Bibliography.

The Vision of Fred
Friend of Poets—
Ami des Poètes

Conversations with
Fred Cogswell
on the Nature and Function
of Poetry

Fred Cogswell and Kathleen Forsythe
With Selected Bibliography by Wendy Scott

Borealis Press
Ottawa, Canada
2004

Canadä

*We acknowledge the financial assistance of the
Government of Canada through the Book Publishing Industry
Development Program (BPIDP) for our publishing activities.*

National Library of Canada Cataloguing in Publication Data
Cogswell, Fred, 1917-2004
    The vision of Fred : friend of poets – ami des poètes : conver-
sations with Fred Cogswell on the nature and function of poetry.

ISBN paper 0-88887-282-8;
ISBN cloth 0-88887-284-4

1. Poetry.   I. Title.

PS8555.O3V57 2004   808.1   C2004-903270-4

Printed and bound in Canada on acid free paper.

To all Fred's friends who he loved
and who loved him

Table of Contents

Growing Up in a House of Poetry 1

Conversation on Writing a Poem 10

Conversation on Finding Poems 17

Conversations on Writing Poetry In English 25

    On the Influence of the King James version
      of the Bible on English Poetry 25

    On the Rise of Imagism 28

    Epigram 30

    On Cadence 31

        Anglo-Saxon 31

        Middle Scots 35

Conversations on the Forms of Poetry 44

    The Romance Forms 44

    Pavanne 46

    Rondeau 49

    Villanelle 51

    Ballade 57

    Ballad 67

    The Sestina 70

    On writing the Sestina: "Essences of
      Green" 73

    On Writing Sestinas 83

    Sonnet 91

    Free verse 103

Conversations On Translating Poetry 106
Conversations On the Art and Craft of Writing . . . 114
Conversations on Editing Poetry 118
Triteness in Poetry 131
The Nature and Function of Poetry 135
A Selected Bibliography of Fred's Work 151

Growing Up in a House of Poetry

For as long as I can remember I have been trained to look at scraps of paper—old envelopes, backs of magazines and newspapers—before I throw them away. It must have come from early childhood when my mother, mindful of my father's penchant to write on the nearest available paper surface, was concerned that my sister and I might scribble on or destroy one of his poems before he had it entered into the typewriter.

I grew up in a house of poetry. Almost every room had bookshelves—the basement was full, not only of books but of boxes of old issues of *The Fiddlehead*. Issues of poetry magazines lay piled in the living room and the study, interspersed with baseball newspapers. Most of the people who came to visit my father were poets or interested in poetry or students of poetry.

I find myself now once again living in a house of poetry. . . . Fred, my father, has left his beloved New Brunswick and come to live in British Columbia and we have made a home together close to his grandson and his family. Again, I am surrounded with bookshelves, the basement full of boxes of his books, checking scraps of paper for poems and entering the poems myself into the computer. Baseball magazines and Fred's record of scores interspersed with correspondence and poetry still litter

1

his desk. I awake each morning to the small sounds of paper as Fred begins his day between 5 and 6 AM—writing. By the time I am fully awake he usually has a new poem, a new translation completed, or even a new book fully sorted. . . . These days he is averaging three books of at least 100 pages each a year.

Thirty-five years intervened between the last time when I lived in my father's house as his child and when I find myself living together with Fred Cogswell once again, this time, not only as daughter but as a grandmother myself. As I write, he is doing the final sort through of the manuscript for *The Kindness of Stars*, his latest (and best, he says!) book. He is careful in the arrangement of poems on the page, in the proofreading of every word . . . testament to the long years of his work as Editor of *The Fiddlehead* and as publisher of Fiddlehead Books.

Just over a year ago, Fred and I sold his home in New Brunswick, packed up thousands of books into a 3-ton rental truck and drove across Canada, taking the northern route through this vast empty land. It was a journey that had come after the death of his third wife and the decision that he was prepared to live here in B.C. with me, close to my family. When I asked him what he wanted to do with the rest of his life, he said that all he wanted to do was write. So this is the life that we lead. Fred has a writing studio with his comfortable chair and low tables in front of him where he can lay out his papers. The books he uses are close at hand. . . . I take care of everything else and we seem to get along just fine. I wryly comment that it must be because I have some of the good features of both his mother, my grandmother, and his first wife, my mother. In the way of families, I do things in the manner he was used to for the first 67 years of his life. It is a great gift to have this opportunity to give back to Fred what he has given to me.

Growing up in a house of poetry, I had no choice but to be a poet myself. . . . Fred encouraged me and published my early works but the lure of family and career took me away from a commitment to creative writing, even though, ironically, writing was to become my strongest skill and the way in which I make my living. However, it was in my interest in learning and how it is we compose meaning that my innate poetic sensibilities have really endured. I call my area of interest the biology of imagination and the language I use regularly involves the 'poiesis' of experience—where I am endeavoring to capture the compositional quality of our living as it emerges moment by moment—life as poetry. For me, imagination is the fundament without which we could not compose our perception of reality. It is no surprise that Fred's child might see the world this way. How else could I think, when as a child, Fred would say teasingly to me, "Now, you need to behave, or I will wake up and remove you from my existence. You are a figment of my imagination."

Fred has already inspired me, as he has thousands of other people, to take out my unfinished books and to write. I, too, now have a studio in our home . . . and I drift between art, craft, writing and the educational work in a creative flow.

For the Vision of Fred is creation and creativity. In the essay: *The Nature and Function of Poetry* that inspired this book, Fred says:

Of all games that life has devised, the most mean-
ingful—and the most bound up with pain and
leisure is creation. Of all the forms of human cre-
ation, the most complex and the one which
absorbs all the attributes of humanity is poetry. It
is like the earth, though. To see it shine at its
most beautiful, we must go to the moon. (p. 147)

So the task of this little book is to take you to the
moon so that when you look again at Fred's poetry you
will see the most beautiful shine.

For the past 18 months, I have been entering Fred's
poems into the computer. He has always written by hand
in an upside down left-handed script which I have learned
to decipher. He has never made the transition to word
processing although his mastery of the typewriter is leg-
endary. I believe he probably typed the original
manuscripts himself for all the issues of *The Fiddlehead*
over many years and all the 307 books he published
through Fiddlehead Books. I know I now have hundreds
of poems in the data file from just the past 18 months. As
I discussed the poems with Fred, I began to observe the
forms that he was using and to ask him about the process
of his own creativity. Although I had known that he
wrote in various forms such as sestinas and haikus, I had
not really come to appreciate the depth of his skill, the
craft of the language, and the extraordinary intellectual
and creative discipline required. Living in close proxim-
ity, I am able to see the true genius of Fred with new eyes.

Fred has called himself a "traditionalist" and really
believes that we should not abandon the past totally in

favour of an unformed present. Much modern poetry
has become free verse and the concept of form and
rhyme is often looked at askance. When I read one of
Fred's sestinas, an arcane and complex form used by
Dante, I am struck by the way in which the form is ren-
dered invisible and what arises is usually a meditation on
a thought or idea that winds around many perspectives
without losing the core—sort of like the double helix of
a DNA molecule. The reader does not need to know the
structure of the form to appreciate the poetry. The
reader probably doesn't even notice that there is an intri-
cate scheme of repeated words. However, how many
people are currently writing in forms of this complex-
ity—all the time? I believe that, when the reader does
realize the architecture of Fred's poetry, it opens the space
for appreciation even wider—like actually seeing the
inside of a cathedral and its soaring heights after having
only looked at a picture in a book.

This is why I wanted to prepare this book. I felt that
it would contribute to a greater understanding of Fred's
poetry and of his vision—both of which I believe have
much to offer to this age. At the end of the essay that
completes this book, Fred says:

Therefore if we behold only machines and stereo-
types, we tend to become only machines and
stereotypes and to atrophy within those areas of
our minds that exist to make us more. If we read
true poems, however, and hence obtain multiple
visions of reality we are generated into feelings,
actions, and imaginative ventures that are bound

to make us—and the society of which we are members—more than we would otherwise have become. If poetry needs any social justification—apart from what it gives personally to its practitioners—this is it. (p. 150)

This theme is underscored in his book *Later in Chicago*, (Borealis, 2003) in which, in the title poem "Henry Adams at Chartres", he alludes to the seminal moment in which "America and its inhabitants were offered an alternative god—this time not human but a standardized machine. . . ."

The composition of poetry can break the standardized machine and shatter stereotypes. As you will read in the essay in this book, Fred offers us an antidote to the world of mass media and standardization:

I would suggest that in a world of conformist advertising and pressures toward conformity, a poet ought to express—primarily for his own satisfaction and understanding—his personal reaction to experience, reinforced by all the knowledge at his disposal and put into forms and contexts which he has, after extensive trial and error, found best suited to his individual powers of expression. (p. 146)

For poetry by its very nature is about the interface between individual creation and Creation itself. It is a way by which we flow together with the Divine.

If the only person moved by the catalytic activity of the poem were the poet himself, I would still say that he is blessed in his creation, for he is a creator, one with all creators since God and Adam, present at the first great naming of things, and carrying on a purpose for which it would not be too egotistical to suppose the human race was created to fulfil. He has not merely taken meekly from life or ran away from it. He has added something new and uniquely his own to the total scheme of things.[1](p. 146)

As Fred often points out, one of the chief dangers of being a poet is to get quite good at something. On the one hand, you cannot be good at something until it becomes a habit. But once it becomes a habit, it is almost impossible for you to deviate from it. You get caught in putting words together in a certain way. This limits the possibilities of putting them together in a different way. Fred believes you have consciously, continually to attempt to vary things which you may not be good at in order to get out of your particular habit. I believe that Fred has found a way through this conundrum. Writing every day has become his habit, and the many forms he uses push him to explore ideas differently. He often says, once he chooses the words and the form, the poem writes itself.

This is the true craft of his genius—his mastery of form does not arise as a constraining habit but rather as

---

[1] The essay quoted was written in the early 1980s prior to the shift in conventions to ensure gender equity. Fred has always been known for his support of women writers.

a scaffold to free his creative vision to soar. And whenever he has no idea for a poem to write, he picks up a book of French poetry and begins to translate, or he starts reading an encyclopedia, waiting until the poems call him. One of the sections in this book that I found most fascinating is how he can "find" poetry almost from any book by going to the essence of what the writer may have written in prose and picking out seminal phrases. (See "Found Poetry" p. 17) Another is the process of how he "finds" the right word to complete a poem (see "On Writing a Sestina" p. 84).

Fred started to write poetry when he was in high school. He started to write by imitating the forms of the poems he liked that he found in his textbooks. As he says, he ultimately learned that poems do not come from outside but from inside: "But this was not wasted time . . . the years I had spent doing this. It's like a person who has practised on a silent piano for years and suddenly discovers that there is something called music, he, at least, knows where to put his fingers."[2]

Fred's early love of poetry and literature led him to a career as a scholar and professor of literature in addition to being a poet, editor and publisher of poetry. Fred's deep knowledge of the structure of the English language and its music is revealed in the conversations in this book on the metrics of the language and the way in which English borrowed forms and styles from other languages. His ability to translate poetry is also remarkable, especially as he does not speak recognizable French, despite

---

2   Fred Cogswell in *Canadian Literature: A Guide*, CMEC, 1986.

being of Acadien ancestry, largely because of a speech impediment in early life. However, both his mother and grandmother were French speaking so I like to put it down to the influence of the true mother tongue in early infancy. I like to imagine my grandmother speaking and singing French to baby Fred, when my English-speaking grandfather was not around, although I do not know if this is true or not. I know I find myself singing to Fred's great-grandson, Ryu, as a natural response and can imagine my grandmother and my great-grandmother singing to baby Fred as well. Regardless, Fred has a gift of translating the poetry of others in a manner that those poets appreciate.

So much has been said about Fred Cogswell and his contribution to Canadian literature, to poetry, to New Brunswick, to the thousands of students he has taught, to the thousands of writers he has inspired, assisted and supported. Few, however, have been able to see the pattern of his poetic life in the manner that we have portrayed in this small book. Few have the history of being a child who carried the bottle as he chased butterflies. Few suffered with him through the deaths and tragedies and the joys and wonder of family life. It is only now that I am beginning to appreciate how he transformed his experiences into the thousands of poems that are his legacy. As an inspiration to those of us who write or dream of writing, he is an inspiration as a true working poet, whose creativity continues to sustain his daily living.

Kathleen Forsythe
March, 2004

Conversation on Writing a Poem

July 1, 2003 – Canada Day, 9:30AM

KATHLEEN: Fred handed me the following poem, written on a scrap of paper in his left-handed script:

IN THE DIVINE WORLD

In the divine world
Earth keeps Seed's strength. Self is sin
Unforgivable.

So I decided to ask him where the poem came from. He opened the book, *RUMI: Poet and Mystic: Selections From His Writings*, Translated from the Persian with Introduction and Notes by the late Reynold A. Nicholson, which he had been reading, and read aloud from p. 95:

GOD BEYOND PRAISE[3]

When beams of Wisdom strike on soils and
clays
Receptive to the seed, Earth keeps her trust:
In spring time all deposits she repays,
Taught by eternal justice to be just.

O Thou whose Grace informs the witless clod,
Whose Wrath makes blind the heart and eye
within,
My praise dispraises Thee, Almighty God;
For praise is being, and to be a sin.

Pointing to the footnotes in the Nicholson's text Fred
also read: *"Rumi regards the whole inanimate creation as
potentially endowed with life, perception, knowledge and
reason". . .*

And, further on,

*"These lines refer to the mystic's "passing away" from his
praise of God through absorption in the Object's praise. . . .
So long as he is certain of existing and acting individually,
he is in effect denying the Divine Unity. According to a
hemistich quoted by Junayd: "thy being . . . is a sin with
which no other sin may be compared."*

---

3 *RUMI: Poet and Mystic: Selections From His Writings,* translated
from the Persian with Introduction and Notes by the late
Reynold A. Nicholson, George Allen and Unwin Ltd. London,
1968

KATHLEEN: And so? In a sense, you went to the essence of what was there and out of that came this particular haiku?

> In the divine world
> Earth keeps Seed's strength. Self is sin
> Unforgivable.

FRED: I went to what I thought was there and it automatically became a haiku because if you write in English it is pretty difficult to avoid writing in haiku as the English language breaks down into pauses of 3 syllables and 4 syllables. In the haiku what you use is 3 and 2 syllables or 2 and 3 syllables, 7 syllables which is 3 and 4 and then 5 syllables, which is 2 and 3. It is pretty easy to wiggle words around so that they do fit that particular pattern. But you shouldn't waste any words and all the words ought to be appropriate to the idea because if you express an idea in a few words which are keys, you will notice that practically all these words are one syllable. When you do that you have a more powerful poem than you would otherwise. You have contrast because, for example, "the unforgivable" is very easy to say and is very fast whereas most of the words are strong and each word is emphasized.

For example, consider when Shakespeare uses the line: "the multitudinous seas incarnidine making the green one red. . . ."

With "multitudinous seas incarnidine," you hardly have to change the position of your mouth when you are saying it. It is just a matter of breathing. With "making the green one red" you have to change the position of your jaws, your tongue and everything else at the end of every particular word. So consequently you have this change of pace. With a change of pace, you almost automatically get a change of emphasis.

KATHLEEN: So the metrics of the language indicate much about how a poem gets written?

FRED: Yes, although most people today simply use a syllable count and do not realize that there is much more to metrics than that. One of the important things in metrics is the ease or difficulty with which you move from word to word which defines a change of pace in your verse when a change of pace is needed.

KATHLEEN: Can you give me an example?

FRED: "The multitudinous seas incarnidine making the green one red". You can't read "making the green one red" in the same way as you do "multitudinous seas".

One of the best lines I wrote, long ago in the early 1930s, was "The self same song the siren sang upon the lonely sea." Here what you have is a combination of alliteration with the "S" and then the contrast of the alliteration, which is the same throughout the line, because every time it is used, a different vowel is used. This serves to cancel out the assonance which balances the too-frequent use of the alliteration and so you get an effect that you would not otherwise have if you had used a different combination of words to talk about "the self same song the siren sang upon the lonely sea".

KATHLEEN: When I hear you explain this I wonder if there is a technical aspect to poetry that most people don't appreciate at all these days?

FRED: That's right. They threw it out the window with a lot of other things that have been thrown out the window. The result is that some poetry is very, very primitive.

KATHLEEN: If we liken it to painting, we have to be able to paint and draw before we can break out of the form of painting. In the same way, we have to be able to understand the language forms before we can break out of them.

FRED: That's one reason why, for example, French poetry today is in such a mess.

KATHLEEN: Because it lost its lyrical architecture?

FRED: Yes

KATHLEEN: If you write in different kinds of form—like this poem that you just wrote which came in the form of a haiku—is it the particular idea or is it the language that triggers whether it becomes a ballade or a haiku or a sestina?

FRED: You need the repetition of certain sounds where words are expressing or emphasizing the same thing. And to get this repetition, one of the ways of doing so is using a form that combines assonance and alliteration on the one hand, with the use of rhyme and a pattern of the number of syllables per line.

In other words, you draw the kind of map in your mind of what pattern you are going to put the poem in. Once you have the pattern, the mind will provide you with the words that fit that pattern and it will also provide a kind of testing to determine what won't.

KATHLEEN: Surely that does not just come by accident? It comes because you have practised writing poems —over many long years?

FRED: Of course . . . over many years, I wouldn't say necessarily they were long years.

KATHLEEN: Do you actually consciously have that map in your head? Is it an architecture—to use a construction metaphor?

FRED: It is an architecture but it is not an architecture that I keep by memory. I very often have to block out over and over and over again the line endings for the villanelle, which are very complicated. I also still do this for the line endings for the sestina, which are even more complicated.

KATHLEEN: Before we go into why these are complicated I want to clarify the metaphor. It is a map because the writing is a journey that you make over an area that you know because you've made the journey many times and recognize the landmarks. The map opens into a new territory. It is an architecture that generates a contained space that you can expand and elaborate upon.

Conversation on
Finding Poems

FRED: Found poetry arose from the habit that various people who wrote in their diaries had about putting down interesting words and phrases that they had heard in conversation. Now conversation can be interesting for two particular reasons. One reason is that people will often say things, when they do not know that they are being overheard, in such a way as is more revealing of their nature. This deserves more serious consideration than just simply a superficial notation because it shows what kind of person they are. A second reason is that much of the conversation of the world is conducted without any thought but simply from feeling and impulse and, often, many colourful phrases become overused. They are overused *because* they are colourful. They often rely upon other parts of speech like puns or parent relationships which are not in reality relationships at all; and mispronunciation of words as in the case of spoonerisms—"It's customary to kiss the bride," and that sort of thing. I will give you an example:

> I heard two women walking upon the street
> One of them said, "He told me it was sloe gin
> But it sure acted fast enough on me."

This depends on a pun. The word "*sloe*" deals with a substance that you use to flavour gin, while "*slow*" means the length of time of the effect of something. The sound "sloe gin" could be either and she, of course, took what was the wrong meaning. It was the wrong meaning that made the phrase memorable!

Because you are using a form that nobody else has used to cast into words you can compose new poetry. John Robert Colombo in Canada is probably the greatest practitioner of this particular account—this art. I once published a book of his called *The Great San Francisco Earthquake and Fire*. Because the diary that he used dealt with colourful events which had not been too much reported, the book was good for two accounts: one, you got an appreciation of the experience involved in a fire, and two, you had another point of view on the history of the American West at a particular time. In this way, this kind of poetry can justify itself.

Today I located a found poem from the writings of C.S. Lewis:

> . . . the sweet air blowing . . .
> from the land of righteousness . . .
> is more gold than gold . . .

I got this because I knew that one of my favourite fantasy writers, George MacDonald, was a favourite of C.S. Lewis as a fantasy writer. I discovered, as I was looking through my books, that in the edition that I have of

---

4   George MacDonald—*Phantastes and Lilith*, Wm. B. Eerdmans Publishing Company, Michigan, 1976.

Phantastes and Lilith[4] by George MacDonald was an introduction by C.S. Lewis.

C.S. Lewis, in this particular introduction explains that George MacDonald, whom he had never met personally, was, despite some lapses in style, one the of greatest of all fantasy writers in the English language. His greatness was pointed out on one specific occasion, that is, that of all fantasy writers, more than any other, George MacDonald emphasized an aspect of life—its goodness—and that he did not advertise it in a dominant or advertising way. Goodness, in other words, was a relationship that you had with the Universe It was good because the Universe gave you everything that you had. You gave the Universe, in turn, everything that you had. If you appreciated that the Universe was good you would do your part and presumably the result would be an acquaintanceship which was more than hypocrisy or mere surface friendship but a real thing that was lasting, and lasting for good as long as you and the Universe remained constant partners. I took out three groups of words from the way Lewis put it in one particular paragraph.[5]

...the sweet air blowing... (Number 1)

---

[5] C.S. Lewis' final paragraph in the Introduction to *Phantastes and Lilith*, with the phrases Fred Cogswell "found" highlighted:
   The deception is all the other way round—in that prosaic moralism which confines goodness to the region of law and duty, which never lets us feel in our face *the sweet air blowing* from "the land of righteousness", never reveals that elusive Form which if once seen must inevitably be desired with all but sensuous desire—the thing (in Sappho's phrase) "more gold than gold"'.

from the land of righteousness . . .

(2) and (3)
is more gold than gold . . .

So I start with three dots . . . to show that this is a continuation of a conversation
"the sweet air blowing"
three more dots . . .

then a movement to another point
"from the land of righteousness"
three more dots . . .

and finally

"is more gold than gold"

with three more dots . . .

So we have a completed sentence

"Sweet air blowing from the land of righteousness is more gold than gold"

Found-Poem (after C. S. Lewis)

. . . the sweet air blowing . . .
from the land of righteousness . . .
is more gold than gold

And what that means, of course, is that Life is fulfilling and worthwhile and to be valued. The problem with this idea is that the modern world thinks very much like the first four or five centuries after the Christian era (the time of Manacheism and Gnosticism) but uses different terms to pretend that it is original about the goodness and lack of goodness and about duty and the lack of duty, etc. etc.

If you applied these particular lines to present-day America —"the source of sweet air and the land of righteousness" you would get something that is "more gold than gold" even. The trouble is they don't believe anymore that there is more gold than gold, they just pretend to.

The result, read this way in the found poem, is almost an inversion of what C.S. Lewis meant and an inversion of what George MacDonald meant.

KATHLEEN: I want to pick up two ideas—one is the notion of conversations and finding conversations; the other is your commentary on the work that you and Jo-Anne Elder did in translating *Conversations*[6] by Hérméngilde Chiasson and how difficult that might have been in translating what appears to be a series of found poems.

FRED: It is found poetry, in a sense. What happened in that particular book is that Chiasson listened for about five years and whenever he found a memorable conversa-

---

6   Hérméngilde Chiasson—*Conversations*, Jo-Anne Elder and Fred Cogswell—translators, GooseLane Editions, Fredericton, 2001.

tion he wrote it down. He divided up the conversations in a way that I don't think I fully understand anymore than he understands. The result is 999 conversations that are between two protagonists. One is male and one is female. This is the book. These conversations, each of them, is put in the original French as he heard them. Fortunately for the translators, who usually learned in college the particular French vocabulary that Chiasson used, (and such people as Jo-Anne and I use) what Chiasson uses as a vocabulary is easier to translate than if we had had to try to translate some semi-literate version of French. In this particular book, you have two academics translating a French academic and under these circumstances the language is more standardized than it usually is and consequently, these sentences can, as units, be understood and appreciated as sentences and units that are worth consideration. You take each conversation or paragraph of conversation to be a particle of the whole process.

Here is another example of how a poem can be found.

The Yellow Slicker: A Convergence[7]

Two old people mentioned in a single day a yellow slicker that existed nearly seventy years ago.

HE: I saw her once only. It was at a football game. She wore a yellow slicker with a hood pulled back over her shoulders as she sang, "Bye, Bye, Blackbird".

---

7 Fred Cogswell—*With Vision Added*, Borealis Press, Nepean, 2000.

She looked so handsome and her voice so fine that I wished I were older than high school and could have asked her for a date.

I can see that sweater as clearly as if it were right here now.

SHE: My brother gave me a yellow slicker with a hood when I went to college. He wrapped it in a parcel and threw it in the train window at Bathurst when I left for Fredericton.

During my first week, I painted the UNB coat-of-arms on the back and took to wearing it at football games. One day, forgetting the sweater, I moved to another section in the stands. When I remembered to go back for it I found that some one had cut out and taken away the coat-of-arms. The slicker was ruined and I was sad because such an awful thing had happened to my brother's present.

I can see that slicker as clearly as if it were right here now.

FRED: Those two people wrote those experiences in letters to me in the same week!

KATHLEEN: You received those letters in the same week?

FRED: Yes.

KATHLEEN: From two different people who did not know each other? Who had never met?

FRED: Yes! That's right.

KATHLEEN: How many years had it been since they had both seen each other?

FRED: Oh? . . . about 60.

KATHLEEN: What fascinating synchronicity! So found poetry is also about the extraordinary mystery of life.

FRED: Yes, exactly!   There is no answer to it really.

Conversations on Writing Poetry In English

On the influence of the King James version of the Bible on English Poetry

FRED:

Lift up your heads, O ye gates, and be ye lifted up, ye
  everlasting doors
And the king of Glory shall come in. Who is the king
  of Glory?
The Lord strong and mighty. He is the king of Glory.[8]

Now this is an example of how the English scholars in the
16th century understood the cadence of poetry that was
being written in Eastern languages. It was the English
translation of the *Bible* that brought this into being.

The leading Biblical translator in England in the
early 16th century was William Tyndall and Tyndall
spent most of his life—he only lived to be 45 when he
was burned at the stake—in translating mainly from the
Old Testament but also part of all the testaments. His
work was incorporated in the study which King James
commissioned Bishop Sworn to produce with such won-
derful success—ultimately.

---

8 *King James Bible* Psalms 24:7

KATHLEEN: The King James version of the Bible?

FRED: Yes, the King James Bible. Now, this is an English adaptation of the technique upon which the form and rhythm of the Bible are founded. It depends upon the combination of repetition and variation of statements; emphasis takes care of mood and thought. Variation by its interplay of assonance and alliteration makes that statement memorable and provides it with a euphony, i.e., an agreement of sound that conveys an attraction on it that it would not otherwise have. That is why it works:

"Lift up your heads" is repeated with variation in the same line "be ye lifted up"

"O ye gates" repeated with variation "ye everlasting doors" which amplifies the poem.

" The King of Glory shall come". This is a statement which invites the question that repeats the statement "Who is the King of Glory?" That question is answered . . . "The Lord strong and mighty. He is the King of Glory."

And so you have an antithesis or a combination "Who is the King of Glory . . . He is the King of Glory" which is a repetition with variation—the "who" and the "he"—held together by each time adding "the King of glory". When you do this, you are writing a language where different parts reinforce each other at the same time–they are enough alike to provide repetition and different enough to provide a movement. You can carry this into many, many different combinations which is what the translators did.

KATHLEEN: What were they translating from? Was it from Greek and Latin?

FRED: No, they were translating from Hebrew and from Syriac and, to some degree, from Greek and Latin.

KATHLEEN: Those languages lent a certain flavour and colour to the English language which was then shaped by it . . .?

FRED: Yes, that is what happened.

William Tyndale (1492-1536)[9]

As much as Shakespeare
William Tyndale
from most common words
formed rare poetry.

There the wise prelates
who burnt his body
miraculously
saw God in his soul.

---

[9] After we completed the book, Fred wrote this free verse poem in honour of Tyndale who contributed so much to the English language and died at the stake for his beliefs. Tyndale wrote the King James version of the translation of the 23rd Psalm: The Lord is my Shepherd.

Psalm and prophecy
incredibly good.
Immortality,
words paid for with blood.

KATHLEEN: When we think of the language of the
Bible, we can see that it then shaped the language of
poetry and literature for several hundred years.

On the rise of Imagism

FRED: Yes, it did—since at least 1600—400 years of
influence. There was a revolt against it in the late 19th
century and early 20th century called Imagism. Imagism
is a way of telling poetry from prose by the choice and
avoidance of words—what word choice you use and the
words you avoid using indicate whether you are writing
poetry or whether you are writing prose.

Abstractions, particularly non-visual ones, are to be
avoided and words that look concrete and have visual
images were substituted in the place of abstractions. In
other words you made it appeal not to the sound, not
even to the meaning but to the eye.

KATHLEEN: Sort of like concrete poetry?

FRED: Yes, I said words that look concrete—words that
used visual images. Metaphor replaced simile. In other
words something was not "like" something. It became
"the something" in a stronger statement. This was a
stronger effect.

If you say "It was like murder", it is a different thing than saying, "It was murder".

KATHLEEN: Is this analogous to Impressionism in painting?

FRED: Yes, it is analogous to a lot of things. This meant that other simple devices could be used to greater effect than had been the case in more traditional poetry. It also meant a more static development of the poem—more like painting than music. The old poetry, like the poetry of the Bible, was based on musical notation. The cadence, you see . . . in the rhythm of the language. In music the striking power enters more slowly and with less unison.   In other words, one was more like music. But painting replaced music, so that the poetry of the early twentieth century developed in the direction of "eye" poetry, of visual images which were clear and could be seen.

You can find all kinds of examples of this sort of approach being used. If you didn't make these particular word choices, the form wouldn't give you the way because the form was not based on syllables. It was based to a great degree on accents, even though the accented verse was one of the earliest features in English unlike French which had no accent.

You can get such images as Yeats uses when he wants to say what's wrong with the world. He throws out a few concrete generalizations and then he gives the picture of the "rough beast" . . . "slouches towards Bethlehem to be born?"[10]

---

[10] "The Second Coming" in *W B Yeats' Selected Poetry*, edited by Norman Jeffares, Macmillan, 1967, p. 99

That is a trick that is better than all the skills that T.S. Elliot used when he wrote "The Wasteland".

KATHLEEN: You feel that Yeats by using the images was able to capture the emotion and the conceptual content, —all—very fast—in one brushstroke, so to speak

FRED: Yes, sort of that way.

KATHLEEN: In an almost Zen-like fashion?

FRED: In a sense. It was helped by the study of Chinese and Japanese poetry as well. The short poems like the haiku and the quatrain, in English, do this also. In these short poems, because of the lack of words, or lack of syllables that you are allowed to use, or whatever confinement is put upon them, you cannot waste words. You have to use words that pull their own weight throughout the whole poem.

KATHLEEN: It takes great discipline

FRED: There is a great deal of discipline and a great deal of ingenuity. Very often, to prove a particular idea, you turn it ironically, just simply by the use of a word or two, as in an epigram for example.

Epigram
KATHLEEN: What is an epigram?

FRED: An epigram is a short witty poem. Sometimes 4 lines and sometimes 2 lines like

I am masochist
What is your vice?

It can be just a sentence, anything that is very short, and very witty.   A lot of this is to be found in all languages. In one of my books, I have one based on what Scotus said. Scotus, the philosopher, was the chief religious person at the court of Charles the Bald. Scotus was an Irishman (which meant at that time that he was a Scot!).   Charles the Bald decided to have some fun with him at his expense. He said to him: "What is the difference between a Scot and a sot?" and Scotus answered "Thought!"

KATHLEEN: (laughing) So that is an epigram!

FRED: A one word one—you usually have to use more than one word to reveal it.

On Cadence
Anglo-Saxon
KATHLEEN: When we talk about cadence, in the English language, how much has the King James version of the Bible affected the cadence of spoken English?

FRED: It depends upon what time you look at.

KATHLEEN: I mean the English that I am speaking now, the rhythm of my language.

FRED: Originally the language of English was a language of stress or accent.

KATHLEEN: It was closer to Anglo-Saxon?

FRED: Yes, I'll give you an example from Beowulf.[11]

"Are you that Beowulf who boasted with Breca,"

Now you use "Be . . .", "bo . . .", Bre . . ." —three alliterations[12] and, in addition, stresses.

"Are you that Beowulf who boasted with Breca,
So foolish to vaunt the skill of your swimming

"foo . . .", "vau . . .", "skil . . .", "swi . . ."

You have two alliterations combined with the two assonances.[13]

"That vain of your valor both of you bade"

"vain . . . valor . . . both . . . bade"

Here you have assonance—"vain, valor, bade" and you also have alliteration vain and valor and both and bade.

---

[11] See the complete poem in Fred Cogswell "After the Anglo-Saxon of Beowulf," *Dried Flowers*, Borealis Press Ltd. Ottawa, 2002.

[12] alliteration—The commencement of certain accented syllables in a verse with the same consonant or with different vowel sounds.

[13] assonance—The correspondence or rhyming of one word with another in the accented vowel and those which follow, but not in the consonants.

"Goodbye to all caution, cleaving the current
Over the dread deeps of the death dealing ocean?"

You have the same rhythm all the way.

KATHLEEN: You also have the assonance and allitera-
tion : *caution . . . cleaving . . . current* and *dread deeps . . .
death dealing.* There is a staccato rhythm in the cadence.

FRED: Yes, this is repeating the rhythm of the Anglo
Saxon.

KATHLEEN: So when we hear children's nursery rhymes
with definite staccato rhythms is this closer to the origin
of English

FRED: It may be.

> "Neither friend nor foe   could prevent that faring,
> The anxious trip   You two took in the water.
> Both of you embraced   the billows in your arms,
> Out there threshing with hands   and gliding
>   through the waves;
> The sea rolled its wave-swell   whipped by winter
>   winds
> And there you two   Toiled for seven nights
> Weary and powerless in the power of the water.
> If his courage lasts   sometimes Fate saves
> The determined warrior   not destined to die,
> Such was my case   as it turned out.
> Nine of the sea-beasts   I slew with my sword.

I have never heard   of a harder fight
Under the arched sky   or in the sea's stream
Waged ever by any   more wretched man;
Weary I won free   from that web of foes.
Finally the foam-race   through the sea carried me
Till I escaped with my life   in the land of the Finns.

FRED: That pattern is a regular pattern even though the number of syllables in each line may not be constant. Certain events occur in them that involve four different phases—the phases of alliteration, the phases of assonance, the phases of stress and the phases of tempo.

KATHLEEN: So this creates a kind of pacing

FRED: Yes there is a pacing in which four kinds of things in terms of tempo and sound accumulate.

KATHLEEN: This is also embedded in English?

FRED: This was the original English to start with.

KATHLEEN: The foundation of the language has this staccato cadence embedded?

FRED: The foundation was taken away, not by the people who spoke the language but by the people who tried to write, like Chaucer. Langland wrote like this:

"*Every maid I met   I made her a sin sign*"

When they tried to write their language down they were influenced by other people who used the language but were more civilized and ahead of them in culture such as the Italians and the Spanish. The result was that you had rhyme everywhere and you had metrical stanzas that played on rhyme. You had great difficulty to work your way back to something that didn't necessarily rhyme. The attack on rhyme, of course, was what caused blank verse.

Blank verse is a count of either stress or syllable, either 5 stresses or 10 syllables. You can work it out either way you want to. When you work it out with either 5 stresses or 10 syllables you have to put variations in it where your pauses are going to be so that there is a variation in the pauses. Even though you are not using much variety in terms of words you are going to keep your English rhythm from complete monotony by the way you stop and start.

Middle Scots

Here is an example when you have to do the kind of "Chaucer-thing". It is from a Middle Scots poem that I have translated:

The Lament of Cresseid[14]

After the Middle Scots of Robert Henryson
O sop of sorrow, sunken into care;
O wretched Cresseid destined for despair,
Gone is your joy and all your Earthly state,
Of all blitheness now you are bereft and bare.

---

[14] See the complete poem in Fred Cogswell—*Dried Flowers*, Borealis Press Ltd. Ottawa, 2002.

There is no salve can heal you anywhere,
Fell is your fortune and fallen is your fate;
Your bliss is banished as your pain grows great.
Under the Earth, god grant I buried were
Where none of Greece or yet of Troy might hear. . . .

FRED: And the poem goes on like this. . . .

KATHLEEN: When you translate from Middle Scots
were you translating from a Celtic language?

FRED: No, Middle Scots was a variant of Northern
Anglo-Saxon.

KATHLEEN: To translate it into current English you
had to maintain the rhythm and the form?

FRED: What I maintained was what it really was. Robert
Henryson, who was a great Scottish poet, was able to
blend the devices of Beowulf with the devices of form in
such a way that he used the same stanzaic rhyme scheme,
he used the number of syllables of the line to keep his
rhythm, and, at the same time, he threw in all the alliter-
ation and assonance that made the stresses anyway!

KATHLEEN: How did we arrive at modern poetry from
this history?

FRED: You have combined the biblical stuff, with the
cadenced verse, and the Chinese and Japanese principles
of writing poetry and the Eastern principles of writing

poetry based on the number of syllables. What the Imagists used, for example, was what they learned from the Chinese and the Japanese on the one hand and what they learned from the Bible on the other.

KATHLEEN: This was where the fusion occurred—the hybridization, which led to modern poetry?

FRED: The hybridization is a strange thing because there is no emphasis from one syllable to another in the Latin language, in the Greek language and in most Asiatic and European languages. As a result syllables were classified as long and short. Various combinations of long and short were worked out in Greek and Latin poetry.

When people tried to write poems in their own vernacular language, of course it didn't fit. It didn't fit because it does not take account of what is called cadence. The word cadence is the beat—the emphasis. Some words in English, some words in German and most Nordic languages, have syllables which are stressed and other syllable which are unstressed. Most of these people conducted their poetry on a four-beat line.

A four-beat line is found in Beowulf or in the medieval adaptations of William Langland in *The Vision of Piers Plowman*. This particular kind of beat used assonance and alliteration and compound words but didn't count the syllables of the lines. It counted the number of beats. It fused the kind of repetition with a kind of variation that the Japanese and the Bible used to emphasize and to give power—not by changing the words but by repeating them with variation. Like "lift up your heads O ye gates". "

What happened was that the original language was not thought of when they thought of forms for the Italian poets and forms for the French poets. They substituted the beats just as the Anglo-Saxon and the Germanic languages had in their early poems.

KATHLEEN: Did they put the actual natural language into the poetry?

FRED: Yes, that's right.

KATHLEEN: Later they tried to adjust the language to the form from some other language?

FRED: Basically—they didn't try to write like that. Chaucer didn't try to write like that when he attempted to add English to the forms of great poetry. He didn't try to write like the Anglo-Saxons before him. He tried to write like the Italians, because the Italians were writing most naturally out of Latin and most naturally out of Greek. Consequently, things grew up to some degree at cross-purposes.

KATHLEEN: Yes, I can see that. I am not sure that people sat down and figured out the forms. They sort of evolved too, didn't they?

FRED: They evolved all right. They were adaptations. You decided that the thing to do was to make a change in the way you pronounced the words when you read them and so you would make the stresses.

The <u>CUR</u>few <u>TOLLS</u> the <u>BELL</u> of <u>PAR</u>ting <u>DAY.</u>
The <u>LOW</u>ing <u>HERD</u> winds <u>SLOW</u>ly o'er the <u>LEE</u>.

You would read in an unnatural form, giving it the length of syllables as if English had those syllables the same length.

KATHLEEN: In a sense, you are reading English as if it were a different language?

FRED: Yes, exactly! You had to do that in order to adapt English poetry to the Latin. You would have to do that to adapt French poetry also to the Latin and to the Greek. This is exactly the kind of thing which kept happening. We were still doing it when we were scanning lines at school.

KATHLEEN: People still read poetry this way! Often people read the Bible this way as well.

FRED: Yes, very often they do. Originally in Latin and Greek poetry, medieval Latin poetry developed due to the influence of these local languages on rhyming poetry in Latin.

KATHLEEN: But there was not originally rhyming in Latin.

FRED: No, it was not originally a rhyming poetry at all.

KATHLEEN: It is funny how the twists and turns in the evolution of language become embodied in the forms.

FRED: The development of poetry represented two or three separate interests and was for a different purpose than for euphony or the beauty of sound. It was important that you get things right if you were dealing with the religion, or if you were dealing with magic or with law because things were not written down originally. They were memorized.

KATHLEEN: Poetry grew out of the oral tradition?

FRED: Yes, "Thirty days have November, April, June and December"—a way of remembering.

KATHLEEN: Perhaps the origin of poetry in the different languages of the world came from being an aid to memory? What about in Chinese poetry - where the calligraphy was itself an art form?

FRED: That reinforced the aid to memory. What happened as well is that since the rightness is associated with the will of God or the gods, there is a sacredness or an authority to poetry that is not given to common language.

KATHLEEN: In the same way that the Old Testament, the first book of the Torah has to be perfectly copied.

FRED: Yes, of course, because you can't fool around with what God says.

KATHLEEN: Because there is something encoded in the pattern . . . which is the magic of poetry.

FRED: Everybody took poetry and made it the form that they used whenever they wanted to preach, whenever they wanted to govern or whenever they wanted to impress with superiority because they had, in essence, a superior form than their own, in which to put their words

Nowadays, poetry has joined the commonality of language by and large.

KATHLEEN: What about the role of poetry in revolution?

FRED: Every religion used it for revolution because every religion was a brain-storm that was supposed to affect other brains.

KATHLEEN: Modern poets like Pablo Neruda writing in Chile were able to say things in poetry that he may not have been able to say directly in public. The same with Chinese poets, or Irish poets at the time of the Irish revolution.

FRED: Many of these countries, particularly the least academic of them, had developed a large crop of semi-literate verse forms published in the vernacular language like the old ballads and the popular songs.

KATHLEEN: And people sang them like the nursery rhyme, "The Lion and the Unicorn," which originally held a political message.

FRED: Of course, you were very often told stories in the form of allegories. The Mother Goose rhymes are full of such allegories.

There was a kind of overwhelming influence coming to some degree from Europe where the people still spoke languages that were related to Latin—such as Italian and French and Spanish

These were the top countries in the so-called civilized world of the time. England was a kind of outpost.

They had their hands full when they tried to write not just poetry but prose. Prose was the toughest of all to try to put into Latin. In Latin you used word endings, cases and vowels and words all from the Greek or Latin. You didn't have any emphasis except length of syllable. What happened when they tried to write was to write the kind of snippets like Bacon or work that various other Elizabethan writers wrote at that particular time trying to construct long sentences in the model of the Latin period.

KATHLEEN: Wasn't that time before the Protestant Reformation, when Latin was the *lingua franca* of Europe.

FRED: Yes, of course it was. Everything was done in Latin and not in the vernacular of the country.

KATHLEEN: The vernacular of the country was not seen as high literature.

FRED: When people like Bacon and Burton were trying to write Latin paragraphs as readers for philosophy or ideas, it bore no relation to the way in which the English talked to one another. English people spoke to each other the way that people spoke in the plays of Shakespeare; more importantly, the plays of Johnson, because Johnson knew more classics than Shakespeare and he had a sense of things that Shakespeare lacked. The man who wrote the first English prose that was really the way prose was written for providing information or judgment, was the prose of Johnson not Shakespeare.

Shakespeare experimented. He used all kinds of different forms of prose. He had a wonderful ear for conversation and he could take off the weaknesses of various parts of speech very well. He was very important in the history of prose. He was also very important in the history of poetry because he did manage to regularize to a great degree the couplet which he used in his plays and in his ceremonial speeches.

Conversations on the Forms of Poetry

The Romance Forms

KATHLEEN: What about these forms: . . . the pavanne, ballade, the rondeau, the sonnet?

FRED: villanelle and the sestina—all come from Romance languages not from Anglo-Saxon at all and they themselves were deliberate attempts on the part of the poets to write closer to the Latin and Greek poets who avoided rhyme. Consequently since all their words rhymed whether they liked it or not, they had to compromise. You use the same words in each stanza but with sufficient variation so that it is not as monotonous as if you wrote couplets.

KATHLEEN: How is it that the English language lends itself to these forms. Is it its Romance roots that allow that to emerge?

FRED: You can put almost anything in the form of the English language because it is a very flexible language. All you have do is find the words that can express the ideas and then arrange the words. The arrangement is the matter that people don't spend enough time on these days.

KATHLEEN: Some aspects of the history of English have looked at the Norman times when Latin, English and French co-existed for about 100 years. This is one of the reasons suggested for the versatility of English. It has multiple words for the same idea. It has the romance word and the Anglo-Saxon.

FRED: They had everything and they dropped nothing.

KATHLEEN: Did this increase the potential of English for variety and helps explain why it is also a dominating language?

FRED: Presumably. Chinese poetry can dominate in the same way because it has multiplied the words so much.

KATHLEEN: It gives great flexibility to the nuances of meaning.

FRED: . . . which means more is required of the Chinese poet.

KATHLEEN: In the Chinese case, the calligraphy—the look of the poem—is also an aspect of the composition.

FRED: The look is also part of the meaning

KATHLEEN: To some extent that is the case in the way we lay poems out on a page.

Pavanne

> *Pavanne: The name of a slow stately dance*
> *of the 16th and 17th centuries*

FRED: The easiest one of all is probably the pavanne. The pavanne is very hard to find out anything about because basically it belongs to music. It's the form of a dance which was most popular towards the end of the Middle Ages and in the beginning of the Modern period. This particular kind of dance had a rhythm of its own. What the French poets, who used it most, got was a form for poetry that fitted the pavanne as dance in its rise and fall and in the process of its rhythm.

What you do is: you write down a five-line stanza— in French, 12 syllables a line and, in English, 10 syllables. The difference in the number of syllables is largely because of the ease or difficulty of getting from syllable to syllable so that the line stands out as consciously being a line. The French need two extra syllables for that as a rule.

Then you write a five-line stanza saying something. Then you take the first line and you operate on it by writing another stanza of five lines, enlarging on the first line. Then you take the original second line and you begin again with that second line, and use five lines enlarging on it and . . .

You do the same for the third line . . . for the fourth line . . . for the fifth line. When you've done that, you repeat the first, second, third, fourth and fifth lines to remind everybody what you started with and how the poem actually goes. In addition, they will remember not only the one line from each stanza, but they will also get the enlargement, too, and the poem will be together in a way in which it would otherwise not be together.

You start a verse that you can write any way you want to. Then at the end, you have already written a verse without trying to write a verse which enlarges upon what you had started with.

KATHLEEN: In a sense, it is like a spiraling circle that expands?

FRED: Yes, that's what it is

KATHLEEN: . . . and it anchors itself with certain key phrases?

FRED: It is very easy to do. Here is an example:

Pavanne: Dog[15]

The will no longer moves the flesh
To leap for field-mice in the grass
Or chase low-flying crows across
The sunlit pasture fields and snap
At shadows with a young dog's jaws.

---

[15] Fred Cogswell—*The Best Notes Merge*, Borealis Press, Nepean, 1985.

The muscles' mastery is gone
That launched his rage at any cur
That dared defy well-watered signs
Of ownership and poke its nose
Upon the ground his maleness claimed.

And though the ears and nose still catch
Keen signals from the outer world
The voice and smells of love are gone
That made his body's ardent wag
One long extension of his tail.

The earth in all its wonder still
Beats inward on his active brain
But he now feebly acts on it
For joints are stiff and muscles tired
And all the air is strangely cold.

Beside the fire the old dog dreams
And in his dreams does what he wills.
His eyes are closed, his twitching limbs
But reflex of the timeless life
Of thought still working in his mind.

The will no longer moves the flesh.
The muscles' mastery is gone,
And though the ears and nose still catch
The earth in all its wonder still,
Beside the fire the old dog dreams.

Rondeau

> *Rondeau: a short poem, consisting of ten, or in an even stricter sense of thirteen lines having only two rhymes throughout , and with the opening words used twice as a refrain.*

FRED: Here is "Soft as a Dove." It's a rondeau

KATHLEEN: Is a rondeau a French form?

FRED: Yes, "In Flanders Field" is a celebrated rondeau in English.

Soft As A Dove[16]

Soft as a dove, above the town
On silent wings the dusk glides down
And where its feathers touched the street
All the harsh outlines of hard heat
Melted, leaving it sepia-brown.

I knew a girl whose silent frown
Better than words, could so melt down
All anger from her features sweet,
                              Soft as a dove.

---

[16] Fred Cogswell—*With Vision Added*, Borealis Press, Nepean, 2000.

A light, a face, a touch like down,
Of soft feathers. These form a crown
On feelings that to us repeat
Live births, so warm, so moist, so sweet.
We grow calm even as we drown,

Soft as a dove.

Soft As a Dove, the first four syllables are a kind of key. As a key they appear three times, "soft as a dove" "soft as a dove," "soft as a dove". It has a five line stanza, a three line stanza plus the repeated key: "soft as a dove" plus another five line stanza ending with "soft as a dove" thus providing the emphasis.

Villanelle

> *Villanelle : a poem of fixed form, usually of a*
> *pastoral or lyric nature, consisting normally of*
> *five three-lined stanzas and a final quatrain,*
> *with only two rhymes throughout.*

FRED: The difficulty with the villanelle is to manage the way it works to keep the poem moving. There are nineteen lines—five 3-line stanzas and a concluding 4-line stanza. The first, the third and the fifth line have to be the same or practically the same—the third, the sixth, the ninth and the twelfth lines have to be practically the same as well. In your final stanza, what was once the first and third lines come together as two lines making a total of 19 lines. This is like a couplet giving a kind of reinforced strength by having two lines used a line apart check in suddenly—one after the other.

The problem, of course, is how do you spread the content in such a particularly flimsy way and go somewhere at the same time. And, it seems to me, it is always a kind of miracle that it does happen. Some of the best poems of their particular kind like "Do not go gently into that good night . . ." are examples of the villanelle

KATHLEEN: That's Dylan Thomas?

FRED: Yes. That's from Thomas.

KATHLEEN: Poets like Dylan Thomas did write in these forms?

FRED: Of course!

KATHLEEN: People tend to think that they did not—that the modern poet invented the structure used.

FRED: Most free verse is easier to translate because sound in language matters less in so-called free verse. It's a lot easier to stay without changing things when you write free verse because it's when you make the first draft for a poem, you can decide that now that you have got it down, you've done it. It's a kind of music that skims the surface of things and describes, in a general way, the tempo, the pitch, mood. If you want to go farther than that, just as if you want to go farther in art than representational painting, you've got to go into combinations that are different and that ask more of you than the combinations you have earlier tried.

KATHLEEN: Isn't that what the craft of the poet is?

FRED: It is one of the things of the craft of the poet. The other craft of the poet is to read and to think and to improvise around the ideas that one arrives at in one's reading and thinking.

KATHLEEN: Looking for co-inspiration from others? But also experience as well…?

FRED: Yes, exactly! To write a poem you have to have an experience and you have to be able to evaluate the experience and you also have to know how to compose words that will encompass the same kind of experience.

In other words you do this in music, you do this in writing—in art. Any art is the same kind of creative process except that the terms and conventions have different names to them. The effect of experience provides the response, and in the case of the best artists is mainly the ability to find what suits them best.

You can find painters who go beyond representation. What they will choose to entertain and what they will choose to omit—because of their choice of representation or omittance—is creating something new, a new combination that has not been created before, in that particular world. Musicians do the same kind of thing.

KATHLEEN: And the dancer. . . . Art as the exploration of the new!

FRED: Yes, partly, but the exploration and expression of the new is not unaware of the old because no particular mode has been completely explored at the time it is abandoned for the new mode. That is partly due to laziness and partly due to the wearisomeness of repetition which happens when the worst features of any particular mode are exaggerated and given praise that they do not altogether deserve at the time when that praise is given.

KATHLEEN: To return to the villanelle I am interested in why you choose to write in the villanelle form.

FRED: I chose the form in the poem "What Song?" because I am playing with two different things—the song of the molecules and what happens to them in a world that is called Lilliput. I had in mind Swift's *Gulliver's Travels*. When you change radically a particular dimension of something, you change the perspective. When you change the perspective, pride, for example, goes out the window when you minimize the achievements, the theatre in which the achievement takes place and the people who achieve. The smaller these things are the less important in appearance do they seem to be. It does the same thing as distance does from the perspective of the eye. When things are a long way off from you they become small and movements become much slower and their importance becomes minimal in the scheme of various things which do encounter your senses. I have taken the song of the molecules and—What is the molecule?— The molecule is one of the smallest portions in which matter is presumably divided as units. They sing a song because we have the song of the spheres. I am dealing with a world of micro-space. By putting music in the form of micro-space I am limiting its importance.

What Song? [17]

What song do the molecules sing
In the world of their micro-space
And to what beings listening

Do spheral rhythms orbiting
Give Lilliput a cosmic grace?
What song do the molecules sing

---

[17] Fred Cogswell *Folds*, Borealis Press Ltd. Nepean, 1997.

And to what thin tune, thickening
A place that is almost no place?
And to what beings listening

Do such sheer ephemera bring
Swift notes that form a minute chase?
What song do the molecules sing

To celebrate a mighty thing
That pumps the pride of minute race?
And to what beings listening

Will curiosity no longer spring
And there be nothing left to trace
What song do the molecules sing
And to what beings listening?

FRED: In other words, if you get something small enough, near enough to disappearing, its importance disappears, its notice disappears. . . .

KATHLEEN: And the beings who notice disappear. . . .

FRED: . . . as well! That's quite true, they become what they behold. So consequently, this is the kind of minimalism that takes away the importance of everything. It is very much a feature of science.

KATHLEEN: What's interesting about the form that you chose, the villanelle—is that by choosing the strict discipline of repeating certain lines in certain patterns you have limited the number of phrases and words that you can use. You are actually taking that language space and expanding it and exploring it in the same way as the idea of the poem is expanding and exploring the micro-space of the molecule.

FRED: I dropped two syllables a line off—I've minimized it, not expanded.

KATHLEEN: I didn't mean expanded the sound and rhythm—I meant that you expanded the idea by imposing the limits and the minimalism of the sound form. In a sense you are doing a paradoxical thing.

FRED: Well, I am doing something that is not paradoxical. You do shorten lines when you minimize the syllables.

KATHLEEN: That is not what I meant by paradoxical. The paradox to which I am referring lies in the content of the poem which serves to expand our awareness of the minuscule, the micro-space—which is a paradox—expanding something infinitely small. That is what I meant. I like this because the poem is about the molecule's song but takes us to the space between which is, of course, infinite. The restriction of the villanelle form frees you to expand the micro-space.

Ballade

> *Ballade: The technical name of a complicated and fixed form of verse arranged on a precise system, consisting of three stanzas and an envoi; there is a refrain that is repeated at the close of each stanza and the envoi.*
> *It has nothing in common with the Ballad other than a common linguistic origin in the Old French* baller—*to dance.*

KATHLEEN: What are the differences between the Ballade and the Ballad?

FRED: They are both poems but they are very different. Both come from the same origin in French but the Ballade (with an e) has no relation at all as a form poem with the Ballad (without the e). The Ballade is a formal poem which fixes the particular images and lines in a rhyme order, a number of lines per stanza, the number of stanza and the number of rhymes allowed. The Ballad on the other hand simply follows the conventions of folk music and varies very much from place to place and time to time.

KATHLEEN: The ballad is more like the folk song ballad that we know?

FRED: It IS the folk song ballad and behind most of it is a story. It does use repetition and refrain in order to emphasize a story which usually does not need emphasis.

It is closer to music in this respect and is the most musical of the various forms of popular poetry written

KATHLEEN: What is the rhyme scheme of the Ballade?

FRED: There were originally two rhyme schemes for the Ballade in its heyday in the early 15th century. One had three stanzas of ten lines each followed by an envoy or dismissal stanza of five lines—making 35 lines. It developed so that most people used it in 3 8-line stanzas and an envoy of 4 lines. The 3 8-line stanza always used the same rhyme scheme and that rhyme scheme did not allow more than three words at once as rhyming patterns.

The greatest poet of the Ballade was one of the poets of the early phase, François Villon, who was probably the most criminal of all poets, and, at the same time, the finest! It had great fashion and became copied in England by Chaucer. Chaucer usually used the 3 8-line stanza and left out the envoy, the 4-line stanza at the end. I do that sometimes. When you have everything said in the first three stanzas there is no use adding the four lines for the sake of completeness.

Chaucer and other English writers used this form. England was the only country where people used the Ballade as a poetic form very extensively. Then there was a silence of about two hundred years in French literature in the Ballade form. It was revised in the 19th century by a French poet, Banneville, and the English poets at the same time began to write Ballades again and have continued to do so. You may use it for funny poetry, for sad poetry. You can use it for almost anything. The rhymes go together easily and are easily found.

FRED: The ancestorship goes back to the time of François Villon who wrote mainly in the ballade. He had two different kinds of ballades but the one that became popular is the one I usually use.

Ballade for an Unrhyming Age[18]

Far from today's barbarity
Inside my soul I walk alone
Revisit all poetry
That in youth I had made my own.
Adolescence in me had grown
From poets of an older time
Verses that still my brain-cells hone.
Is it merely because they rhyme?

Far from today's barbarity,
In my soul verse lines led me on
To a world wonderful to see
And a hope that has not quite gone.
That world I took and hope still own,
Thereby adding another time
And knowledge of a nobler zone.
Is it merely because they rhyme?

---

[18] Fred Cogswell—*With Vision Added*, Borealis Press, Nepean, 2000.

Far from today's barbarity
Inside I place upon my throne
The gentler creed of chivalry,
The human longing to atone
In love, let others' worst be known.
No more men aim at what's sublime,
They read prose now, let verse alone.
Is it because they do not rhyme?

When power lies in property
And machines pollute the time
And we read prose not poetry
Is it because we cannot rhyme?

KATHLEEN: What is the structure of the Ballade?

FRED: The structure basically is three 8-line stanzas and
one 4-line stanza and the rhyme schema for the 8-line
stanza is **abab bcbc** for the first three stanzas and the last
4-lines allows more freedom and you can use alternate
rhymes if you want to. You should repeat something that
was in the other first 3 stanzas. What I repeated was "is
it merely because they rhyme?" Each time, it is done in
a different context and with a slightly different nuance. It
is not as good as this one.

KATHLEEN: What makes one poem, in your mind,
better than another such that you say "This one is better"?

FRED: Because of the way that the problem that has to
be surmounted to get the poem written.

KATHLEEN: Which is . . . ?

FRED: What are you dealing with.

KATHLEEN: Do you mean the idea? and the emotion?

FRED: Yes.

KATHLEEN: Whether or not the form, and the structure and the metrics support the idea and the emotion?

FRED: Yes . . . here is a different one.

Earth, I Have Always Made My Prayer[19]

Earth, I have always made my prayer
A good excuse for work begun.
I took with thanks your food and air
And struggled to deserve your sun.
What matters is what I have done,
Not whether folk praise me or weep.
I want to die with my boot on
And not slip away in my sleep.

Earth, I have always made my prayer
With knowledge I was only one.
What others did was their affair;
I had to trust them and be done.

---

[19] Fred Cogswell *With Vision Added*, Borealis Press, Nepean, 2000.

And though my strength is nearly gone
I yet would rather work than weep.
I want to die with my boots on
And not slip away in my sleep.

Earth, I have always made my prayer
To let wind blow and waters run.
The energy everywhere
Is joy enough for everyone
To share. I neither fear nor shun
The fact that these things will not keep.
I want to die with my boots on
And not slip away in my sleep.

Earth, I have always made my prayer
For now and let the future keep.
I want to die with my boots on
And not slip away in my sleep.

KATHLEEN: That shows the repetition and how the repetition can be used to support the idea.

FRED: Yes. That's it.

Possibilities[20]

What if this world's a giant egg
Whose shell has begun its shaking,
Taking world-enders down a peg
Or two, finding there a breaking
Of barriers, a time of waking
The new life, aeon hatched, under
Earth's core, an energy-making
Too great for our drills to plunder.

What if this world's a giant egg
Spawned by lust and greed, a caking
Pollution around a thin keg.
So the pressure grows, it's aching
For one last error, the breaking
Which signals a final blunder
When the slimy world-quaking
Mess dissolves in blood and thunder.

What if this world's a giant egg
On which we feed, a thirst-slaking,
Gut-stretching appetite. We beg
Borrow, steal, and murder. Taking
All we can grab there and making
Nothing for payback. I wonder
How long before the sun's baking
Will fry what's left of it under.

---

[20] Fred Cogswell *With Vision Added*, Borealis Press Ltd. Nepean, 2000.

Great Prince, who owns every egg
In all worlds over and under
Let your new one hatch now, I beg,
But in it for power put wonder.

KATHLEEN: and one I have chosen . . .

Ballade of Winnie the Pooh[21]

When I was young I read Winnie the Pooh,
That clumsy bear with honey-hungry claws,
Christopher Robin, Eeyore, and young Roo.
Now I am old, I heed more adult laws
And have less patience with children because
They do not do the chores that should be done
While they applaud the things which Tigger does
Each time he thinks he is the only one.

In Kanga, Mrs. Mouse, and Owl, my view
Soon detected some outrageous see-saw
I would not have had such strange creatures do
Had they been mine and I their author was.
Different chaws fit different jaws
And they often find the first taste forgotten.
Did Tigger know himself as now he does
Each time he thought he was the only one?

---

[21] Fred Cogswell *With Vision Added*, Borealis Press Ltd. Nepean, 2000.

And yet is there really so much to do
That we should ask a playtime beast to pause
In what it's doing for an hour or two?
Because we fear its solipsism flaws
A playtime world that allows no laws
Except its own idyllic sense of fun?
Let every beast do what it best does
While Tigger cries, "I am the only one."

Hail Prince, and rejoice. Let us view
Loosely, all we see in the land of fun
Pin Eeyore's tail on! Get stuck with poor Pooh!
Leap like Tigger, when he's the only one.

KATHLEEN: I wanted to ask you about the metrics because it is interesting that even though there is a structure to the rhyme scheme, if I were to write this down as prose would it also pass muster? You could write it as sentences.

FRED: No, I don't think it would because you see there are different units in sentences.

KATHLEEN: How much is rhythm part of the poem?

FRED: Very much, because every line is a unit. It gives a picture or a part of a thought at that part where the thought is throughout the line unless you shift it in the middle for reasons of variety or emotion. Unless you do this, what you've got is a unit.

KATHLEEN: Often in a number of your poems you address Great Prince. Who is Great Prince?

FRED: Great Prince is Dear Reader . . . because in those days poetry was important and it was written to princes giving them advice because it was after all the oracle by which people lived.

KATHLEEN: So, in a sense, what you do in your writing in addressing it to Great Prince is oracular. Great Prince is being oracular . . . being a medium for wisdom. . . .

Ballad

> *Ballad: originally a song sung to the rhythmic*
> *movement of a dancing chorus.*
> *Now applied to popular and romantic verse*
> *that is often sung as a folk song.*

FRED: Here is an imitation of Bliss Carmen.

October[22]

After Bliss Carmen

With a hood of purple berries
And a cloak of gay attire
Comes the gypsy maid October
To set the hills on fire.

She's a kiss of scarlet colours
On a mouth that sumac dyes,
And her frosty touch is magic
To the blue of Autumn skies;

For it tempts with tang of clear days
An Earth grown drab and old
To have one fling at living
Ere Winter come and cold.

---

[22] Fred Cogswell *Dried Flowers,* Borealis Press Ltd., Ottawa, 2002.

So the green turns gold in burning
Or flaunts in orange fire
Where the dying leaves determine
To have a splendid pyre.

An though you fly no banners
Nor blazon bright in view,
The gypsy maid, October,
Will work her will on you.

With a breath of vine-sweet fragrance
And a wisp of early frost,
She will tease your tired senses
Till their jadedness is lost.

She will charm your heart from boredom
With her vivid reckless mood
Till the old mad zest of being
Goes coursing through your blood....

In days of listless languor
When the cyder apples fall
Comes the gypsy maid, October,
To break the Summer's thrall.

KATHLEEN: What is the format that you are using?

FRED: It's a ballad.

KATHLEEN: Not a ballade, but a ballad?

FRED: The difference is that the ballad is set in a 4 or 8-line form and it usually has a chorus and has rhymes. It is the folksong of the English language from the Middle Ages. Here is one that is more my own than "October."[23]

A Ballad of Orchard Evening[24]

Out in an orchard evening
They walked without a word,
And apple buds in moonlight
Above them swelled and stirred.

Out in an orchard evening
They walked through apple bowers,
And on them fell the honey
Of gently swaying flowers.

Now back from orchard evening
They come without a word,
But deadly hangs the silence
Between them like a sword.

And lips that kiss at parting
Are now a hail-hard shower
To bruise and shred and mangle
The fragments of a flower.

---

[23] Fred Cogswell *The Kindness of Stars*, Borealis Press Ltd. Ottawa, 2004.

[24] This particular ballad has been set to music by Janis Kalnins and was recently aired by the CBC as part of a tribute to the late New Brunswick composer.

The Sestina

> *Sestina[25]: a poem of six six-line stanzas with an envoi in which the line endings of the first stanza are repeated but in a different order in the other five.*

KATHLEEN: You mentioned that the sestina and the villanelle have more complex lines.

FRED: That's quite true. In the sestina you need a 6 line stanza to begin and you take it from there according to the rhyme scheme worked out by the late medieval and early modern poets, Dante and Arnaut Daniel. [26] You write that down as a six-line stanza and then you map out the line endings for the rest of the poem which go according to the scheme, which you can find out by looking in the *Encyclopedia Britannica*. There will be five more stanzas—so there will be six stanzas of six-lines and then you have a capping stanza of three lines which is like the twist of two lines at the end of a Shakespearean sonnet but which sort of really gives a twist to the whole poem up until then by emphasizing the real importance of the poem. You can use it as a poem itself much the

---

[25] ses-ti'-na, —a lyrical fixed form invented by Arnaut Daniel, a Provençal poet of the 12th century and used by Dante and Petrarch, distinguished by its six six-line stanzas (originally unrhymed), its six end words repeated in a different order in each stanza, and a three- line envoy in which are distributed these six words, three in the middle and three at the end of the lines.

same way as you might use a haiku simply to give a strong general statement at the end,   stronger because you have already illustrated the details before you come to it and so the person who reads it is in a mood to receive that particular closing.

KATHLEEN: My particular feeling when I read the sestina is that it is like a flowing sculpture in space, which is both a conceptual sculpture and a sound sculpture. When I use the word sculpture I am using it as a dynamic and not as if it were fixed in space. It has that same quality of flow.

FRED: You can do certain things that you can't do with a haiku or other forms of short poetry where the shortness and the formal demands have to combine with the thought whereas in it you can combine things that aren't usually combined. You haven't much competition because there are not too many sestina writers in the world.

KATHLEEN: And you have written a lot of them. Why did this form attract you so much?

FRED: Largely because it seemed to suit me.

KATHLEEN: To write a good sestina you have almost to swallow the form so it isn't obvious at all?

FRED: That's true. What you have to do is to be as careful of your diction in the sestina as in prose in order to write a poem of the length of a sestina.

KATHLEEN: So if you were to take the same sestina and write it as a paragraph it would be probably be seen as poetic prose?

FRED: Very much! It is responded to as prose as it is seen as poetry.

KATHLEEN: Yet because it has this internal composition, it is really a very disciplined form of poetry.

FRED: It is that.

KATHLEEN: Because you conserve the structure, everything else is free to change so it does provide an architecture for freeing meditative thought.

FRED: The point is that it shifts the architecture in the direction of a certain vocabulary. By limiting the words that fit into the structure of the poem, that vocabulary as it builds up adds thoughts that suit something in the mind that makes it easy to arrive at the thoughts that agree with the original vocabulary with which you started the poem .

KATHLEEN: So the coherence reveals itself! In its own circularity!

FRED: Exactly!

KATHLEEN: That's very interesting. I have friends who are painters who choose a palette limited to 3 or 4 colours and then explore those. In the same sense you are taking six words and then exploring the space those six words generate in conceptualization.

On writing the Sestina: "Essences of Green"

FRED: I started to write a sestina and I picked six words "green," "portion," colour," "glass," "other," and "rain" and I wrote the first six lines.

KATHLEEN: Did you pick those six words at random? What triggered them?

FRED: No, they were not random. What triggered them was that they ended each line of a landscape I looked at in my mind.

> Water and sun mingled in proportion.
> Between them they caught the glint-shine of glass
> Softened by the faint blur of almost rain.
> Since nuances absorbed one another
> The eye, caught by the strength of one colour,
> Remembered the world in a short word, green.

And then I've written another line

"Of all the spectrum's hues the one word, green,"

But I want to point out that what is not covered by any scene that deals with landscape because in terms of what is actually seen physically you would need many words to catch what was actually there in the green. However there is one reason why *green* is used and that is that all these words that can be made up to mean *green* have to come from chlorophyll and the seeking of the light of the sun that the land creatures have. That's the beginning.

KATHLEEN: This is the beginning of the poem and what the poem will be about? You see in your mind's eye a landscape. . . ?

FRED: Yes.

KATHLEEN: and you begin to describe it in words. The landscape is deeper than a visual landscape. In a sense, as our painter friend was saying, you could look at one place and paint it for the rest of your life.

FRED: Yes, you could.

KATHLEEN: Every time you look you are seeing it with new eyes . . . as your vision deepens.

FRED: That could happen. I haven't got that far yet.

> "Of all the spectrum's hues the one word, green,
> Is at best a unit whose distortion . . ."

Now the next line has to end in "colour"

KATHLEEN: This is how it goes. The words trigger a set of ideas

FRED: Yes. That's right.

KATHLEEN: Then you explore the language around those ideas?

FRED: Yes, yes . . . the meaning

KATHLEEN: . . . and you fit it into the rhyme scheme of the sestina . . .

FRED: Sure . . . It's very simple.

KATHLEEN: (laughing) I don't think so!

Fred went back to work for an hour.

KATHLEEN: You have four more stanzas now?

FRED: Yes. . . . the first four.

> Water and sun mingled in proportion.
> Between them they caught the glint-shine of glass
> Softened by the faint blur of almost rain.
> Since nuances absorbed one another
> The eye, caught by the strength of one colour,
> Remembered the world in a short word, green.
>
> Of all the spectrum's hues the one word, green,
> Is at best a unit whose distortion
> Is necessary. There's not one colour
> In our perception, but, clearer than glass,
> Function shines; chlorophyll and no other
> Builds the bridge-world between sun and rain.

There difference disappears as the brain
Subsumes a hundred hues and calls each green.
As when one vision starves another,
Fat perception dwindles thin proportion.
That makes us wonder what we see in glass
Or what it is we can learn by colour.

Even when we close our eyes, the colour
That we want to see, be it sun or rain,
Or something unnoticeable as glass,
Is only what our reflection's green
Has raked up out of our mind's proportion
In motley heaps for time's dust to smother.

KATHLEEN: How's it going?

FRED: That's two thirds of it nearly.

KATHLEEN: When you concentrate, how are you
unfolding the idea?

FRED: The idea is being unfolded so that you see that
there is no truth that is guaranteed in the way we see or
in the way we think.

KATHLEEN: You got to that idea through unfolding
the patterns of these words? It is a kind of meditation,
isn't it? Writing sestinas is a poetic meditation.

FRED: Yes.

As I read I wish that thoughts are other
Than they are and let my eyes see colour
As it is, undone by disproportion
In a war between sharp sun and blurred rain
That blinds me to realities of green
And the particularity of glass.

It is an irony. What is brain's glass?
Words there are at odds with one another
So much that we lose a live world of green
From our vocabulary, lack colour
To feel full energy of sun and rain
That gives the wide world its true proportion.

I know I need another proportion.
I shall not perceive but be sun, rain, glass
Not colours but the true vocabulary of green.

It's called "The True Vocabulary of Green".

KATHLEEN: You didn't know that until you got to the
end.

FRED: That's right.

KATHLEEN: In a sense it is a circular process.

FRED: The last line of the body of one of these sestinas
has the same rhyme ending as the first line has.

KATHLEEN: How easy was it to write this poem?

FRED: Very easy.

KATHLEEN: It took you about two hours. When you are writing are you lost inside the idea? You were quite focused.

FRED: No, I'm not lost. I'm looking for words that give me ideas.

KATHLEEN: How do you look for them? In your mind?

FRED: I have them written down.

KATHLEEN: Oh, I see, you make your rhyme scheme and then you fill in the words.

FRED: Yes!

KATHLEEN: Ah! You take the six words, write the first stanza, and then you take those same words and put them in the sestina order and then find the words that will fit those line endings and unfold the idea? It 's sort of like a DNA molecule back to front!

FRED: Sure. The words supply themselves . . .

KATHLEEN: . . . once you get the rhythm and the notion.

FRED: The logic of this poem is quite good, I think.

KATHLEEN: I think it is an amazing intellectual exercise and an emotional exercise too because it has to do with . . .

FRED: . . . It has to do with the fact that if you can't trust a word like "green" what can you trust?

KATHLEEN and FRED: (spontaneously) What can you trust! Is there nothing sacred!

FRED: . . . except perhaps Being and all the consciousness of objects has that and the energy of objects has Being. This is a kind of detour or blinding alley that takes our energy away from our living.

KATHLEEN: The notion of us habituating "green"?

FRED: The notion of us thinking that we have mastered something like colour, for example. We have not. We haven't even looked at it.

KATHLEEN: ... at the level we need

FRED: . . . to know anything. In other words it's not meaning but Being that matters.

The next day

KATHLEEN: Last night I typed up the poem and it was called "The True Vocabulary of Green " and today its called "The True Essences of Green". What happened over night?

FRED: Well, I scrapped the word 'vocabulary' for a couple of reasons. I had to have the word "another" in here to fill out the requirements of the verse and so consequently I had to keep *another* and when I put the *another* in "I know I need another proportion./ I shall not perceive but be sun, rain, glass. . . . It was not the vocabulary I wanted it to be, it was not the names, but these things . . . as they are.

KATHLEEN: . . . as they are.

FRED: Right, not colours but the true *essence* of green.

KATHLEEN: The first time the circularity was that you didn't know it was the vocabulary of green till you got to the end. Then, when you slept on it, on reflection, you realized that it was not the vocabulary at all but the essence of green.

FRED: That's right.

KATHLEEN: You used the vocabulary to get there but it was the essence that was the meaning.

FRED: That's right

KATHLEEN: Are you happy with it now?

FRED: Yes, I am much happier with it.

The True Essences of Green[26]

Water and sun mingled in proportion.
Between them they caught the glint-shine of glass
Softened by the faint blur of almost rain.
Since nuances absorbed one another
The eye, caught by the strength of one colour,
Remembered the world in a short word, green.

Of all the spectrum's hues the one word, green,
Is at best a unit whose distortion
Is necessary. There's not one colour
In our perception, but, clearer than glass,
Function shines; chlorophyll and no other
Builds the bridge-world between sun and rain.

There difference disappears as the brain
Subsumes a hundred hues and calls each green.
As when one vision starves another,
Far perception dwindles thin proportion.
That makes us wonder what we see in glass
Or what it is we can learn by colour.

Even when we close our eyes, the colour
That we want to see, be it sun or rain,
Or something unnoticeable as glass,
Is only what our reflection's green
Has raked up out of our mind's proportion
In motley heaps for time's dust to smother.

[26] Fred Cogswell *The Kindness of Stars*, Borealis Press, Ottawa, 2004.

As I read I wish that thoughts are other
Than they are and let my eyes see colour
As it is, undone by disproportion
In a war between sharp sun and blurred rain
That blinds me to realities of green
And the particularity of glass.

It is an irony. What is brain's glass?
Words there are at odds with one another
So much that we lose a live world of green
From our vocabulary, lack colour
To feel full energy of sun and rain
That gives the wide world its true proportion.

I know I need another proportion.
I shall not perceive but be sun, rain, glass
Not colours but the true essences of green.

On Writing Sestinas

FRED: " The Beach at Noon"—This is a sestina that is a part of *Meditations: 50 Sestinas*. When I was writing this I was spending a great deal of time in Prince Edward Island on the beach recovering from the death of my first wife. "The Beach At Noon" is one of these poems in which I tried to pin down—if you ever can pin down— exactly what your relation is to consciousness and to a particular kind of consequence in this place, in this way. So I start out with the beach . . .

The Beach at Noon[27]

Full-faced to the brisk sea gale, I breathe air
Cold, sharp, and salt as the white-edged waves
And see the same sea-silver on gulls' wings
That slip the driving wind. Above me now
The sun's noon glory hangs, reminding me
There is some brightness that no eyes can bear.

On the bay's other side the cliffs are bare,
Then sudden flower in the lambent air
Rose-red against the double blue of waves
And sky. But even as I watch them now
Their glow already seems less bright to me
Who in this moment feel my lack of wings.

---

[27] Fred Cogswell—*Meditations: 50 Sestinas*, Ragweed Press, Charlottetown, 1986

Fixed on this spot even as the wind wings
Up cloud and shape-dissolving rain. I bear
The pain of seeing now a scene I know
I am a part of patterned in the air
With all of air's fragility—cliff, waves,
Sun, sky, gull wings one instant fused in me!

Although the core of consciousness is me,
The power is otherwhere. Outside are wings
Of wind and gull, are sun, cliff, sky, and waves
That, despite my hope and memory, bear
Their kaleidoscopic patterns in the air,
Intent upon an ever-moving *now*.

I command a world within, active now
As words and symbols weave their spells for me,
But it's tied too tight to the outer air
By sense impressions, and the flying wings
Of every thought are lipped by the bare
Hard knife of fact that around them waves.

It is when my current and the world's waves
Blend in one billow, as they did just now,
That their imbalance is so hard to bear.
There is this difference between things and me:
Things know no pattern; like chaff winnowings
They drift wherever force directs the air.

On wings of wind, the rain-squall drives the waves.
The air above grows dark. Outside me now
The discord lays my limitations bare.

KATHLEEN: Why did you choose the sestina as the form in which to write these thoughts?

FRED: Because I started out with the first six words. . . . . Having started out with the same six words, I had to use the same six words in different order in all the next stanzas and then put all six them all in the last stanza.

KATHLEEN: The words are "air", "waves", "wings", "now", "me", "bear". Then they show up in this sequence . . . bare . . . air . . . waves . . . now . . . me . . . wings in the second stanza and then throughout the endings of the other stanzas in the poem. When you read the poem you do not notice this rhyme scheme at all.

FRED: I know—you do not have to notice it because it is part of the regular rhythm of English.

KATHLEEN: That's what interests me about this as a form—It is a meditation in some way because it does have an internal structure but the structure is invisible.

FRED: That's right. It should be invisible.

FRED: The rhyme scheme of the sestina is as follows . . . based on any 6 words that you choose as the original a,b,c,d,e,f.

Stanza 1
a . . . air
b . . . waves
c . . . wings
d . . . now
e . . . me
f . . . bear

Stanza 2
f . . . bare
a . . . air
e . . . waves
b . . . now
d . . . me
c . . . wings

Stanza 3
c . . . wings
f . . . bear
d . . . know
a . . . air
b . . . waves
e . . . me

Stanza 4
e . . . me
c . . . wings
b . . . waves
f . . . bear
a . . . air
d . . . now

Stanza 5
d . . . now
e . . . me
a . . . air
c . . . wings
f . . . bare
b . . . waves

Stanza 6
b . . . waves
d . . . now
f . . . bear
e . . . me
c . . . winnowings
a . . . air

The 3-line envoi uses three of the end-words in three lines at the end of the poem. The other three end-words are interspersed elsewhere in the envoi.

On *wings* of wind, the rain-squall drives the *waves*.
The *air* above grows dark. outside *me now*
The discord lays my limitations *bare*.

KATHLEEN: There are fifty of them in the book, *Meditations*.

FRED: There are probably about another hundred or so in different places.

KATHLEEN: It is a discipline to learn to write this way! Do you just pick any six words and then start?

FRED: Yes!

KATHLEEN: What happens to the words? Do you really have to struggle? Or does it entrain itself?

FRED: What happens is that the first six words unite new words with them which move the poem forward.

KATHLEEN: So the words themselves are coherent- in a network so to speak?

FRED: Yes, they enlarge the network.

KATHLEEN: Once you start shaping it like a sculpture then it falls into place and you just sort of have to "tweak" it?

FRED: Yes . . . here's one . . . "To Hesiod" . . . Hesiod was the Greek pastoral poet who wrote one line which is quoted in John Galsworthy's Collected Works *The apple tree, the singing, and the gold.* It's an English translation of the Latin.

To Hesiod[28]

In Spring, when I was young, the apple tree
Above my head had blossomed white as snow.
Its fresh, clean smell suffused the air. I felt
The world was one with blood and nerves and skin
When through the boughs the sun beamed joy
Upon the grass in dancing motes of gold.
And there I lay and heard the sounds of gold,
Round notes that fell like petals from the tree
As in the branches a brown bird threw joy
My ears were quick to catch and hold and know
As sometimes special, ever held within
The cells that hold whatever 's deepest felt.

The birdsong ceased, but still my keen ears felt
A gentle susurration where the gold
Bees murmured; their constant, low-pitched zin-zin
Came drifting down from blurs of industry
In flowers where the swift-winged workers now
Had found the honey that their hives enjoy.

Scent, song, bees, and bloom were but half the joy
That on that morning then my senses felt.
The other half was something I know now
As being one with these live things; all gold
It seemed was spendthrift *now* before the tree
Leaves learned that they could fall in time's dust-bin.

---

28 Fred Cogswell *Meditations: 50 Sestinas*, Ragweed Press,
Charlottetown, 1986.

I went back once to where my youth had been
One cold Fall day and found but little joy.
Stripped of its leaves and blossoms was the tree.
The bees were hived against the cold. I felt
No kinship with crow-caws. The ground was gold
With muddied leaves, and in the air was snow.

The fact that I was one with these was now
A thing that I regretted more than sin.
Time turns the spendthrift into miser; gold
Is most desired when most rare, and the joy
Of life becomes more precious when less felt.
The tree of knowledge is a bitter tree.

Despite what then I felt, what now I know.
Your lines bring back the joy that blazed within:
"The apple tree, the singing, and the gold."

KATHLEEN: The inspiration was that last line. Then
you unfolded the idea and the feeling you had about it
back until you reached the last line again?

Sonnet

> *Sonnet: a piece of verse properly expressive of one idea consisting of fourteen decasyllabic lines, with rhymes arranged according to one or other of certain definite schemes*

KATHLEEN: We talked about the sonnet. The sonnet is one of the few forms that people still study at school and they remember that Shakespeare wrote sonnets.

FRED: The earlier version was the Petrarchan sonnet and in the Petrarchan sonnet the English version finally came forward—one if its practitioners was John Milton. You used two parts to the sonnet—the octave—the first 8 lines. and the sestet—meaning the last 6 lines. In the octave, you asked a question, and in the sextet, you answered it. Or you made a proposition in the first 8 lines and in the last 6 lines you put forward another proposition or you quarreled with it. There was a kind of balance between the beginning and the end and when the last line is written one can see the balance.

Now rhymes were allowed to tie together each of the sections in a particular way—*abba abba*—that's the first section. You could change the second stanza to **acca** if you had difficulty finding rhyme schemes sometimes. Then in your last 6 lines you were given almost complete *carte blanche* as to what rhymes should occur. Usually there are three rhymes paired in such a way that they do not follow consecutively

The second kind of sonnet, the so-called Shakespearean sonnet, is a sonnet form that Shakespeare used in the poetry that he wrote. He used three 4-line stanzas, or quatrains followed by a concluding couplet. You have either a positive ending of that kind or a kind of negative ending that tosses away what the first twelve lines do in favour of a new approach at the end. It gives you an option so you don't always come to the same conclusion. You get a greater chance of variety when you attack the proposition than you would have if you did not have this alternative.

KATHLEEN: Some of the early poems that you wrote in the 1950s were sonnets about people that you knew from your youth. You found this form suitable for what you wanted to say?

FRED: I found this form easy and suitable. It's quite easy to tell a story in 14 lines because you use the characters at a particular point in their emotional development that catches the past, present and future of their lives. The sonnets are like snapshots. These particular snapshots ought to be sufficiently striking such that the moment that you read them you see what you are supposed to see. It ruined me for writing fiction! If you can write a story in 14 lines why would you use 200 pages .

KATHLEEN: And yet, that is not to dismiss fiction?

FRED: For me, it dismissed the storytelling part as far as I was concerned.

KATHLEEN: I know, I had to relearn how to write fiction after being a haiku poet. After learning to see things in 3 lines it is difficult to expand ideas into 300 pages!

FRED: The reason why I am talking about the sonnet at this particular time is that the one thing that is absolutely essential or necessary to the writer and the reader is empathy. How the writer reveals people as struggling or not struggling or doing what they will with their environment is the life that is produced by words.

These people as people did not exist but they are, in a sense, symbolically everybody, because in many aspects, each of them encompasses existence, in terms of feelings and in terms of habits and customs, in terms of instincts, in terms of the limits that are put by the whole physical nature upon consciousness. Consequently when you have such a thing it is good that everything can become equally real in the mind.

Democracy[29]

Joe Benson and his wife would fight and smash
The windows of the small tarpaper shack
They lived in right behind the railway track
Then make it up, and if they had the cash,
They'd both of them get drunk on bootleg mash
And stay that way until their money went.
Unless they earned it, no one gave a cent
To them who always were and would be trash.

---

[29] Fred Cogswell *Immortal Plowman*, Fiddlehead Books, Fredericton, 1969.

But suddenly a day would come when she
Was given credit at the Elder's store
While Sunday-suited men in cars would go
And dare the mud before the shanty door,
Trying with money, drink and flattery
To buy Joe's vote, worth more to them than Joe.

When I was twelve years old I used to read James
Fenimore Cooper dealing with the noble savage, Nattie
Bumpo (except he was a white savage. That's why he
was noble, and the other types of savage were not consid-
ered quite so noble!). When he was put in the stocks in
New York State around Cooperstown I cried because I
felt for the poor devil very, very much. At the same time,
when I read William Shakespeare's "Hamlet" and I came
across the actor putting on the fake play to arouse the vil-
lain, the actor was so aroused by the play that he wept.
The fact that empathy is so recognized was a wonder to
Shakespeare and I think it ought to be a wonder to us all.

Here is a sonnet:

Act of Love—For William Shakespeare[30]

Although the space between us lies immense,
There floats across the void from him to me
The fine-spun gossamer of poetry
Drawn from the entrails of experience.

---

[30] Fred Cogswell *A Long Apprenticeship: Collected Poems*,
Fiddlehead Poetry Books, Fredericton, 1980.

Not like a web that catches flies by chance
And lets them wither to oblivion;
This is an act of love whose touch is one
With all of mind and muscles' nervous dance.

A Trojan plain, the sound of martial drums,
A withered crone, face torn by grief and fear
Amid the press of Grecian victory.
No need to ask the question now: "What's he
To Hecuba that he should weep for her?"
I read, and in my tears the answer comes.

The first two quatrains of the sonnet, the octave, follow the outline of a Petrarchan sonnet—*abba acca*— then the final six lines, the sestet.

The opening is an outline of the relationship that lies between the writer of something and the reader of something and of poetry. This is exemplified by detail that comes directly out of "Hamlet" and it is commented on as a marvel by Hamlet himself as he watches the actor weep over someone who never really existed.

KATHLEEN: There seem to be many, many layers in this poem.

FRED: Yes, there are.

KATHLEEN: To appreciate the poem you also need to have an appreciation of Shakespeare.

FRED: Yes, you do need this.

FRED: The other sonnet I have chosen is a Shakespear-
ean sonnet.

There are Two World's In Time[31]

There are two worlds in time; one dark, one light:
In circling stasis each on other preys,
Where all between the poles of black and white
Revolve or spiral through their nights and days.

When you behold the blind and silent worm
Become a song inside a robin's throat,
Or see in Spring an orchid blossom form
Its own sweet scent from slime that feeds its root,

Think how in turn a worm will feed as well,
One night to come, upon that robin's meat,
Or how the root that gave will canniball
And care not if the bloom be foul or sweet;
And realize, then, unlike flower, word, bird, slime,
Your thoughts of time have put you outside time.

FRED: The idea is that there are these two worlds of
time and you get caught in them—the dark world and
the light world that prey upon each other—and when
you see them become a song or an orchid blooming out
of the slime—we have that Buddhist hymn OM MA
NE PADME OM—and the eye in the lotus? Think how
in turn, a worm, or a robin, or a root, becomes a canni-

---

[31] Fred Cogswell *A Long Apprenticeship: Collected Poems,*
Fiddlehead Poetry Books, Fredericton, 1980.

bal—these things are done. And what we call sweet and what we call foul are not permanent at all. What is permanent is not the flower, the worm, the bird, the slime —but the thoughts of time that put you outside time.

KATHLEEN: In choosing the way you wrote this as a sonnet, you took the form where there is an argument presented and then turned on itself.

FRED: Yes, I turned it around completely. I start with *two worlds in time—one dark one light.*
  This is the normal way by which people usually look at things—good and evil, and so on—or permanent and temporary. Ultimately what is written down is not good or evil, it's not permanent or temporary. It is not finite. It is infinite and timeless.

KATHLEEN: The Shakespearean sonnet gives you a form to explore the whole idea?

FRED: Yes, and you can use these forms anytime when you write sonnets. All you have to do is work at it.

KATHLEEN: When Shakespeare was writing his sonnets, this is what he was doing even in the structure of his plays?

FRED: Oh yes!

KATHLEEN: We often don't notice they are sonnets because they are built into the flow of the dramatic structure.

FRED: That's true. Probably the best sonnet writer in the world was a French 19th century poet called Maria José de Heredia. As far as translating sonnets, a great many sonnets have been written by Émile Nelligan. Edmund Wilson, the American critic regarded Émile Nelligan as the first modern poet.

Nelligan wrote no poems beyond the age of 18. Most of his life, after that, was spent in a psychiatric ward, and in a sense, that is the position which traditionally the modern poet was assigned to occupy after the French poet, Rimbaud. What was modern about the poets from Rimbaud on is that to an increasing degree they became alienated from life as they had been taught by the education system and by the practical world of affairs. Alienated from that particular world, they attempted to show their alienation. Madness is a form of alienation. Whether or not Nelligan was mad or not, "Tawny Landscape" is a landscape of sustained beauty where Nature is harsh, colours are few, temperatures are cold, life is hunger and yet, in that night (and nights are long and days are short) in that night, Light has a brighter shine where it does exist. It is not necessarily regarded as evil because if people are used to night, they often delight in it. So we have a sonnet translated from the French.

Tawny Landscape[32]
After the French of Émile Nelligan

On a high cliff where the horizon rose,
Stand the trees, like old men by rickets bent
Or damned souls under the whips of torment,
Twisting in despair their fantastic torsos.

It is Winter; it is Death; on Arctic snows,
Flogging their horses at break-neck pace
To far-off camps where still their fires blaze,
The hunters ride, chill beneath their heavy clothes.

The north wind howls; it hails; night falls in gloom;
See how suddenly through the shadows loom
Savage packs of wolves, through starvation bold.

Stiff-legged they leap; in tawny swarms they rise,
And the stark horror of their burning eyes
Lights the white loneliness with sparks of gold.

FRED: In a sense, this is a lovely universe. But it is a dark, cold, hostile universe. On the other hand, there is a satisfaction in existing and overcoming and eating. The less you eat, the hungrier you get. What he has caught is a sense of alienation. What poets had been taught and what civilized people had been taught was to value their lives and so we run into the exact opposite.

---

[32] Fred Cogswell *Deeper Than Mind*, Borealis Press Ltd. Ottawa, 2001.

He lived in Montreal. His mother was a very Christian woman. He was very fond of music, the music his mother played. The home he lived in was gentle. His father was away from home. He was an Irish-Canadian postal official. Ultimately, he attempted to cure Nelligan by sending him off to England on a boat. Nelligan rejected the boat, he rejected business and then he failed his exams, which was his last resort—he had led his class up until then. Finally he just simply became an inmate of one of these Catholic institutions that looked after insane patients.

KATHLEEN: When you look at this sonnet, it says "After the French of Émile Nelligan"; is it a translation or is it a new poem?

FRED: It is the equivalent of an Émile Nelligan poem in the English language.

KATHLEEN: In other words, what he had to write in French in the sonnet, you had to write in English as a sonnet. You had to know how to write English sonnets. So it is not a literal translation but rather a translation of form following the inspiration of the other poet.

FRED: Yes, you could say that.

KATHLEEN: What would you say was the driving force in your love of poetry . . .

Note: *Fred responded to this question as he did to most questions of this order by picking and reading a poem—as*

if it must be self-evident from the very sound of his words,
which, unfortunately, are not reproducible. You, the reader,
may choose to read these aloud yourself.

FRED: "To Tongue's Surprise" which owes a little bit to
the present poet laureate of the world.

KATHLEEN: Who do you mean?

FRED: The Irish Nobel Prize winner, Seamus Heaney . . .

To Tongue's Surprise[33]

To tongue's surprise no taste is ever dumb.
It can't withstand the leaf's willow-dapple.
Nor the rich barbed thrust of crab-apple.
Wild taste offers unexpected freedom.

From comb-clogged wax I feel strong honey come.
The mild ripe seed of caraway caressed
My mouth as dry as a late Fall harvest,
My jaws made a good chew out of spruce gum.

Tang of tansy and cool mint. Such things blend
To build a rare, inexplicable end
Where two extremes meet enough to be real
As they return to justify impulse;
One is cold water in raw oatmeal;
The other, purple-salt-royale called dulse.

---

33 Fred Cogswell *Dried Flowers*, Borealis Press Ltd., Ottawa,
   2002.

FRED: It's about the tongue's surprise and it is a sonnet.

KATHLEEN: Inspired by Seamus Heaney. . . . ?

FRED: In a way because he writes this kind of poetry. He sometimes writes in sonnets. . . . He writes very well.

Free verse

> *Free verse: Poetry that is based on the irregular*
> *rhythmic cadence or the recurrence, with*
> *variations, of phrases, images, and syntactical*
> *patterns rather than the conventional use*
> *of meter. Rhyme may or may not be present*
> *in free verse, but when it is, it is used*
> *with great freedom.*

KATHLEEN: What would be the difference between blank verse and free verse?

FRED: Well, blank verse is based on the ten-syllable line.

KATHLEEN: Iambic pentameter?

FRED: Yes, and it corresponds to the 12-syllable line in French.

KATHLEEN: So it is the rhythmic metric of the language that makes the distinctions?

FRED: In that kind of metric. It is not the only metric in the language.

KATHLEEN: What are other metrics?

FRED: Accent, for one thing.

KATHLEEN: How we "swallow" words, for example.

FRED: How we change the words according to the difficulty or the ease of pronunciation . . .

FRED: Most free verse is easier to translate because sound in language matters less in so-called free verse.

KATHLEEN: You do write in free verse?

FRED: O yes, many poems such as this one:

The Senses[34]

My mind opens the windows of my eyes
and I see you standing straight and clear
although you are

                  miles and years away

When memory moves the inner ear
deep inside

                I hear your voice
and smile with sudden joy

And sometimes in a vacant room
the familiar scent of you

                now and then
as from a flower breathes

---

[34] Fred Cogswell *A Long Apprenticeship*, Fiddlehead Poetry Books, Fredericton, 1980.

But what my mind loves most
the touch and taste of you
                              is dead
except through masks of other women

Conversations on Translating Poetry

KATHLEEN: In translating poetry, what are you really doing?

FRED: In translating it, I am rewriting the poem using the same words in English.

KATHLEEN: In a sense, when you translate poetry from any language you are trying to maintain the integrity of the original poem in a new language?

FRED: Yes, Here is one called "Pot-Pourri", or dried flowers.

Pot-Pourri[35]

On a white page all the words wait in line
Full of forgotten light that makes us find
The last relics of a lover's goldmine,
Poems remain, dried flowers of the mind.

KATHLEEN: I like that image.

---

[35] Fred Cogswell *Dried Flowers*, Borealis Press Ltd., Ottawa, 2002.

Can we look at a poem that you have translated from French? It seems that going from Middle Scots to English seems less of a stretch than going from French to English.

FRED: It is. . . . Here is a poem called "The Crows" by Émile Nelligan.

The Crows[36]
After the French of Émile Nelligan

In my heart I saw a flock of crows in flight,
Crowding that inner pen in gloomy bands,
Great crows from peaks renowned in many lands
They flow by in the moon's and torches' light.

Like a circle our graves, a dismal sight,
That has a zebraed-carrion-feast discovered,
In the ice cold of my bones they hovered,
Waving in their beaks shredded hunks of meat.

Now, this prey ripped for these night-devils' yield
Was merely my tattered life where ever still
Vast enemies arrived converging on it,

Pitiless, tearing with great pecks of every bill,
My soul, a carcass strewn on the daily field,
That those old crows will devour bit by bit.

---

[36] Fred Cogswell *Dried Flowers*, Borealis Press Ltd, Ottawa, 2002.

FRED: Here is a modern free verse poem

This Day[37]
After the French of Alain Grandbois

Walls that hold
The darkness the Unknown
This and that they told us
And gave us dirges for our very own

Joyless   where no hope blooms
Sin is ordained
And burning souls enchained
Where are the bright rooms

What you are what deep within you gnaws
No one knows   you do not know yourself
Blessed revolt   your strongest firmest oath
Nothing can stifle its laws

The sea's dumb waves swelled in a motion
And the world crumbled he said she said
All this is just a futile notion
We are already feloniously dead

Glory of lineage   thirst for life
Cruelty under love's roofs lurking to leap
Walls of the last day mighty and deep
This knot of keys that sets our wits at strife

---

[37] Fred Cogswell *Dried Flowers*, Borealis Press Ltd, Ottawa, 2002.

No, no no entry
Walled villa   beware the dog at the gate
What matters our fate
We are tied to Eternity.

KATHLEEN: Now you have translated that poem from French. There seems to be a certain level of rhyme in it. Did you put it there or was it there in the original?

FRED: It was there in the original. Most of the time, they don't bother making it happen in French. Here is a different kind of poem

We Must Play Well[38]
After the French of Jacques Godbout

There are children in the Sahara
Without toys made in the U.S.A.
They make themselves
But since they have no paper nor scissors
And no paints and paste
They take bones
The bones of wild dead camels.

KATHLEEN: This is a very powerful image . . . as you said earlier about how the image controls the poem.

FRED: Yes, it is a powerful image. Here is one that is different again.

---

[38] Fred Cogswell *Dried Flowers*, Borealis Press Ltd, Ottawa, 2002.

The Little Church[39]
After the French of Olivier Mercier Gouin

The little church in fact
Has yielded to the times
Its stones are moss-attacked,
Its beadle is humpbacked,
Its curé's purse is packed,
And through its windows, cracked,
A breeze is humming rhymes.

FRED: There are no people in it . . .!

FRED:

Tortoise[40]
is not a stone
is not rewarmed in sunshine—
It moves.

KATHLEEN: Is this haiku a translation or is this your own?

FRED: It is an alternative of Jocelyne Villeneuve's haiku.

La tortue[41]
Une pierre
se réchauffe au soleil—
Elle bouge!

---

[39] Fred Cogswell *Dried Flowers*, Borealis Press Ltd, Ottawa, 2002.
[40] Fred Cogswell *Dried Flowers*, Borealis Press Ltd, Ottawa, 2002.
[41] Jocelyne Villeneuve *La Saison Des Papillons*, Éditions Naaman, Sherbrooke,1980

KATHLEEN: In this poem the title becomes part of the poem?

FRED: Yes as in:

Snob[42]
The humming-bird
flies by here and flies by there
without seeing me.

Snob[43]
Le colibri
ole par ici, vole par la
ah, sans me voir

KATHLEEN: She has done this in all the haikus you have translated of hers. To be able to translate her haiku, you have to be able to write haiku in English. Haiku is so much about image.

FRED: It is a form of imagism. Of course it was imagism that arose from Ezra Pound's translation from the Chinese and Japanese which lead to the formation of Imagism of which he was one of the chief apostles.

---

[42] Fred Cogswell *Dried Flowers*, Borealis Press Ltd, Ottawa, 2002.
[43] Jocelyne Villeneuve *La Saison Des Papillons*, Éditions Naaman, Sherbrooke,1980.

Story of the Heart[44]
The highs and lows—
like the fountain's water-jets
Life has ups and downs

Histoire de Coeur[45]
Des hauts et des bas—
Le jet d'eau de la fontaine
jaillit puis retombe . . .

KATHLEEN: When you are translating haiku like this what does it actually feel like? Is it like writing an original haiku? Or is more like doing a crossword puzzle?

FRED: A little of both. I like crossword puzzles, too.

KATHLEEN: When you do haiku, there are only the 17 syllables so how do you arrange them?

FRED: I usually arrange them as 5, 7, 5 and I usually throw a rhyme in.

KATHLEEN: Do you maintain the French poet's particular order?

FRED: It depends on whether I change the order—on what best lends itself to English.

---

[44] Fred Cogswell *Dried Flowers*, Borealis Press Ltd, Ottawa, 2002.
[45] Jocelyne Villeneuve *La Saison Des Papillons*, Éditions Naaman, Sherbrooke,1980.

KATHLEEN: You try to keep the image.

FRED: I try to keep as many of the same words as possible.

Conversations On the Art and Craft of Writing

KATHLEEN: Fred, I know that you've been a very good typist although you did not make the transition to the computer. Even though you did not, I noticed that you have always written your poetry in longhand first. Has that always been the case for you?

FRED: It has always been the case for me.

KATHLEEN: You have not composed directly through the keyboard. Do you think this makes a difference and in what way?

FRED: Yes, in a way, you have time to write the stuff.

KATHLEEN: I know that I prefer to write creatively in long hand although I can also compose directly to the word processor. I think there is a different process going on in the different forms of composing.

FRED: Well I have to make sure these things keep all the forms that I have for them.

KATHLEEN: And you can't do this with a machine.

FRED: Oh, I get mixed up every now and then these days, even writing.

KATHLEEN: The other thing I wanted to talk about is the process of thinking about a poem that you are going to write. Do you think about poetry all the time? When you get up in the morning and you start writing, do you just start? Do you have to make yourself start?

FRED: Mostly I just start but sometimes I have to make myself write. It depends on how fast you are writing. If you are doing an awful lot of poems, you have to start thinking fairly early in the morning about it.

KATHLEEN: Well, many people feel they write poetry when they are moved by inspiration. For you it's a daily activity—a discipline in that sense. I'm trying to get at the creative process—whether or not you wake up with a poem in your head or whether you have to inspire yourself to write and how you do this.

FRED: Sometimes I have one partly in my head but I don't usually remember it very well.

KATHLEEN: Do you read to inspire yourself?

FRED: Some

KATHLEEN: Do you play with words?

FRED: Some. . . . I do anything that will help.

KATHLEEN: Do the translations also become part of this? They are part of the on-going discipline.

FRED: I've lost some originals—and I don't know what these translations are!

KATHLEEN: You mean you don't know what you translated?

FRED: I've got to find them; some of them are here and some of them are not.

KATHLEEN: You probably have 3 or 4 books going on at the moment—a very large amount of poetry. Has this been the norm for you throughout your life?

FRED: No, publishing other people's poetry![46]

KATHLEEN: Yet you also had lots of poetry- if the poems weren't yours they were somebody else's.

FRED: Yes, I've always had lots of poetry around because I had to read all the poems when I was Editor of *The Fiddlehead*, and when I was Editor of Fiddlehead Poetry books.

---

[46] Fred Cogswell was Editor of *The Fiddlehead* from 1952-1966 during which time he reviewed thousands of poems. He was the publisher of Fiddlehead Poetry Books from 1955-1981 during which time he received hundreds of manuscripts, which he reviewed and to which he responded. He published 307 poetry titles during that time. He currently publishes through Cogswell Books which released one title in 2003.

KATHLEEN: You've always been surrounded with poems?

FRED: Oh yes!

KATHLEEN: How do you find it when you read someone else's' poems. Do they trigger poems in you?

FRED: Not very often.

KATHLEEN: You're quite clear about this distinction?

FRED: Yes.

Conversations on Editing Poetry

KATHLEEN: For the past fifty-odd years, you have spent much time involved in editing—first of all *The Fiddlehead* magazine and when you published Fiddlehead Books, you received thousands of manuscripts. As the story goes, you did not just reject peoples' poems and manuscripts, you took care and time to respond to each one with suggestions for editing. Many people have referred to you as being their mentor and editor and a recent journal dubbed you "Friend of Poets." What does it mean to edit—to edit your own poetry and to help other people to edit?

FRED: In my own poetry, as a rule, I try to save myself trouble by writing on whatever subject interests me. When I do, however, I am usually taking some pains not to thrust my particular idea or conviction onto the reader. I try to present a picture and allow the picture to modify the reader's impression in the direction I want. Poetry is a form of propaganda. Propaganda is also about religion and has the good and the bad qualities of a religion. If handled properly it can transcend the simple application to the things in life. In other words you can say more than what events signify but which has somehow or other worked into your own subconscious by

118

using experiences and reading. This goes into the poems one writes, such as sonnets.

KATHLEEN: When you look at poetry that someone has sent you, written in the sonnet form, and you want to give them some editing advice, are you looking for how well they have used the form?

FRED: Yes, although I am also looking always in poetry for more than that. If they don't use the form, they can be taught and they can improve very much. What I am looking for is whether or not what they are writing means something to them. You can tell by reading it whether they are just simply aping something else, or trying to take a subject or a technique that happens to be fashionable, or trying to interest people by shocking. In other words going beyond the natural medium of things in poetry—the kind of thing which sometimes succeeds with editors.

KATHLEEN: What does succeed with editors, given that so much of modern poetry is free verse and is not written in form?

FRED: What succeeds is advertising and money!

KATHLEEN: You mean people pay the editor to get their poems published?

FRED: They do not necessarily pay the editor but they go to editors who are working for whomever has the money to do the publishing business.

KATHLEEN: I can see that people who want their work published go to a company that has the resources to publish poetry.

FRED: There is another reason of course. I began Fiddlehead Poetry Books with a company in England which at the same time operated a magazine called *Trace*. *Trace* was a magazine which was the agent of Villiers Press and also attempted to preserve what it considered to be the quality of poetry. The result was that it had very good people working for it in England and in the United States. My connection with them meant that there was a whole availability of poetry—some of the best in Britain, some of the best in the U.S. that went to *The Fiddlehead* magazine, when I was editing it.

KATHLEEN: Is this how *The Fiddlehead* became an international magazine and not a magazine local to New Brunswick?

FRED: Exactly right. As far as support from the rest of Canada went, New Brunswick would never get it. When I got support from the United States and from Britain, it couldn't exactly be ignored.

KATHLEEN: So we are never recognized in our own backyard? It is only when someone from somewhere else recognizes the significance of what we are doing that people pay attention.

FRED: This is true because the mind works this particular way. When you think of the great poets of the past who have their reputation solid and secure you presume that the people who came from the same place are still writing to these standards. So if you get published in Great Britain or if you get published in the United States, it is something. Whereas if you get published in Canada, you have to deal with people who think that Toronto or Vancouver is the centre of the world.

KATHLEEN: I think this exists in other countries as well, not just in Canada.

FRED: It still exists in places like France with respect to recognition of women poets and to poets writing in French from outside France. It continues to exist in English with respect to women poets. The difference may be in the difference in the social habits of women as compared to the social habits of men. Poetry in England and Europe in general was the pursuit of men who had a lot of time to spend in pubs drinking and talking and gossiping. Often men were very lazy about their profession as poets. This was also true of Canada. When women got going and joined the League of Canadian Poets and established the Feminist Caucus they put everybody to work writing serious poetry.

KATHLEEN: That was a good influence then! Let's be specific about what you do when you receive poetry from people. Most of it would be in free verse. How did you respond to them, about whether you were going to publish them or not?

FRED: I could show them how they used too many words. I could also show them how they did not have rhythm fitted quite right. I also tried to tell whether it was more for show than anything else was.

KATHLEEN: I remember as a fifteen year old saying I wanted to write poetry and asking you for advice. You gave me a book of haiku and told me to try writing one and to remember to take out everything I didn't need. I have always remembered this as the dictum: take away everything you don't need.

FRED: You can write quite good poems using haikus as stanza forms.

KATHLEEN: I also began to write poetry which was a series of haikus. I found that in my own writing I would often write a poem in free verse and then edit it to take out everything I didn't need and arrive at a haiku every time! I eventually trained myself to see in haiku!

FRED: At the end of the sestina, you will find three lines at the end of each sestina, that are very much like haikus.

KATHLEEN: What about people who write in form? Out of the thousands of manuscripts you have reviewed and responded to, how many were written in the different forms we have been discussing? Let's take haiku out as many people do write haiku. Did you receive many sestinas, villanelles or ballades, the forms we have been exploring in this book?

FRED: Not many. . . . Only a tiny percentage even tried to write in form. That is one reason why poetry has gone backward. It's less memorable because the aids of memory—repetition, rhymes and use of the same rhythm throughout—have basically gone by the way.

KATHLEEN: Do you think there may be a flickering interest in form growing?

FRED: Yes, I see faint flickers. The same faults are made everywhere as are made in Canada. All those who write a poem think that the way they have written it is original. Since everybody is very different from everybody else that would cut out a lot of people from being poets. Many people who try to be poets these days do not succeed because the choice to go around and find what they can do tells them they are expected to do what somebody at school or university expects them to do.

KATHLEEN: Most people will admit that at some point in their life they have written a poem.

FRED: True, but they usually got discouraged. There are many examples. Loren Eiseley, one of the greatest sociologists was also a poet. He started out as a hobo and he became a sociologist by studying many courses. He took one English class and he wrote one essay. The professor called him in and told him that the essay was too good for him to have written it and then failed him for plagiarism! He never took any more English and became a leading poet of his century.

KATHLEEN: Last year, you were corresponding with a young man who wanted to go to university and he was writing formal poetry. He seemed like an anachronism from the 19th century and I wonder how he will fare in the 21st century university?

FRED: His poems are much better than most people's poems are. I do not think he will get a welcome reception. That is because most editors are hungry and they behave somewhat like rats.

KATHLEEN: You are very hard on editors, having been one for so many decades!!

FRED: I read a review recently of a book which maintains that a particular publishing company discovered Alden Nowlan. Well, I know that there were a number of companies that had published Alden before they got to this company. I was one of the first. The problem is that publishers only look at themselves and not at the wider context.

You begin to realize after all the meetings I have attended that the publishing industry is about the publishers getting money for themselves and credit for themselves and they sometimes fooled with the facts in order to get it.

KATHLEEN: As a child, I remember the visits to the house and the time you spent with Alden. For you, editing seems to be much more than writing a critique and letter. It involves deep personal friendship, a recognition and validation of the other poet's worth and legitimacy, a mutual respect.

FRED: As far as mistakes go, I am afraid many were made. For example, why did T.S. Eliot turn down *Animal Farm* and put George Orwell in such a difficult and awkward financial position? That was in 1944.

KATHLEEN: And Doris Lessing sent out her book, *The Diary of Jane Somers*, under the name Jane Somers to see whether the publishers would recognize the work of a "new" author.

FRED: The same thing happened at the time of Trollope. He wondered about this whole business of publishing. So he published a couple of novels under a pseudonym and nobody paid any attention to them so he went back to writing under the name of Trollope again!

KATHLEEN: And George Eliot had to take a man's name to be taken seriously and published!

FRED: True.

KATHLEEN: Can you comment on what you see now as the state of poetry publishing in Canada?

FRED: Well, the state of publishing is still as awful as usual. The state of writing is better than that. The complicating factor has been the standardizing process that teachers of creative writing have inflicted on students who in turn have become teachers of creative writing and have inflicted on their students.

KATHLEEN: There is a vicious cycle beginning?

FRED: There is a cycle going on of this kind and I am concerned that it serves to cut out as many people as it encourages. It gets good writing, true, but it also gets writing that is not good, that is not sincere. I am not sure that this is the best way to teach people how to write.

KATHLEEN: When I was going to school, we were taught sonnets, Shakespeare, various forms. We were not encouraged to write these. They were taught as historical artifacts, as great literature. Nowadays, there seems to be a complete absence or inclination that you could write in something other than free verse.

FRED: It is the growth of specialization such that what people get to know is more and more minuscule. It is done in the interest of standards, I suppose. I remember people who wrote theses on various writers. They would write them on one novel or one aspect and they would never read anything else but those writers and sometimes they only read one or two selections of the particular author's work. They were specialists on a particular person and a particular work and were only vaguely aware of anything else.

KATHLEEN: This seems a limitation.

FRED: Of course it is a limitation. This limitation is now in almost every art in the world—over specialization.

KATHLEEN: The days of the "Renaissance" person— (although Hildegard of Bingen preceded the Renaissance!) when people did many things—they wrote music, poetry, operas, painted, did science, discussed philosophy because they considered this part of being learned. Do you see this returning in any way?

FRED: Now and then . . .

KATHLEEN: I find in your poetry a great resonance with systemic and systems thinking, both fields in which I am involved that cross many specializations. It is about the interconnectedness of everything. Your poetry integrates rather than separates into specializations. Do you have any further comments on editing prose or poetry?

FRED: The problem of editing prose which is also true of poetry is that you have to establish faith. That is to say, you have to generate a mood in the reader so that the reader will take what you say on faith and listen to it. When I say listen, you listen not just with your mind, you listen to the images, to the choice of images, to the words, how they suit, to the particular tone. You listen to what people listen to when they hear music, notes and how the notes are put together. When the notes go together what you have at the close is what music is trying for, when you get this same quality in poetry or fiction then you get what poetry or fiction is trying for—a kind of oneness or unity in which all the elements involved, dealing with something that has to do with life, fit together.

KATHLEEN: When I am writing a novel, even though I am writing in fantasy, I have to create a believability, a coherence in the world that I am generating. This is the same case with the poem. It has to generate a coherence within itself that the reader can believe in.

FRED: One of the problems now is that so little is known by people that it is almost impossible for people to form their ideas about anything

KATHLEEN: In the novel I am writing, I am generating many co-existing dimensions in an attempt to have people break out of the hold that the wallpaper of social reality traps us in. I am writing this to expand people's awareness of the way we can perceive our world. Poetry has this ability as well.

FRED: Yes, it does.

KATHLEEN: Why does poetry endure, Fred?

FRED: When a poet has succeeded and produced something, just as a painter or a musician has, if he or she has really done it, and that has been established over a long period of time, there is a value that he or she accrues from history. People are proud of their history. In every country there are periods of history that are considered better than the present.

KATHLEEN: So writing poetry gives people hope?

FRED: Yes, it gives hope.

KATHLEEN: Poetry written in the extremes of war, revolution, personal and natural disaster gives people an expression of the emotion that is collective—it becomes the voice of the soul of a people. Fiction does not often do this. Do you think that it is the way in which the language of poetry opens the space to the heart?

FRED: There are many things that open the space to the heart. Anything that is well done opens the space to the heart, everything from painting and music and poetry to a good golf swing.

KATHLEEN: You are right! Is it something about coherence with Life?

FRED: If you look at dance or music, to reduce things to the minimum necessary motion is to improve them. If you don't know how to dance, you go every which way. If you don't know how to play a game what happens is that you learn to unite what you are doing with something else that is involved in the doing of it so that there is a timing or a coherence between the things. During the course of this the use of unnecessary energy is discarded.

KATHLEEN: This is the discipline. When you write in forms, the discipline actually frees the mind to explore the idea.

FRED: It takes a great deal of discipline and a great deal of work.

Triteness in Poetry

FRED: The ancient Greeks have a story bearing on one of their customary institutions in self-government—banishment. A state could hold elections and collect signatories. If enough signatories were available a person could be banished from a state in which he was a citizen. Greek government got rid of many trouble-makers in this fashion, but the system was not fool-proof. For example, Aristides, one of the greatest citizens of Athens, was banished by the vote of a blind man who asked him to enter his name for banishment. The philosopher asked why he was acting in this way. "Oh," said the voter, "I'm tired of hearing him called the just."

This reaction occurs often when we encounter phrases which are mentioned more often than the market for quotations can comfortably bear. I think in a way children sense this in their drawing and use of colours and shapes that do not belong to themselves but to their own caprices. I first noticed this when I looked at your colour work and I wrote a poem about it. Transposing too-often used words, clichés, to different words, where, freed from trite associations, the reader would get a different impression. I used this device in "The Dragon Tree" to employ the same words in a new context so they would be fresh again.

The Dragon Tree[47]

Strange-scented birds and song-flowers grow
In the garden where I cannot go,
Where green-trunked trees grey apples hold
And bluefish swim in pools of gold.

And always there a green sun grows
To burn the song of the red-leafed rose
While yellow grasses bend their knees
Before a blue-bird-smelling breeze.

Around the garden's circle flies
The dragon-tree to eat the skies
With silver-scented food that sings
Hid in the branches of its wings.

That garden now to me is gone
Where sight and sound and sense are one,
But children walk there still before
They eat the gardens cherished store.

Many years later, when I was a good deal older I carried
this tradition farther in a poem called "The Apple Fancier":

---

47 Fred Cogswell *A Long Apprenticeship: Collected Poems,*
Fiddlehead Poetry Books.1980.

The Apple Fancier[48]

In whatever shapes or sizes
he loved them for the life
that glowed beneath their skins.

But the world in which he lived
had its own peculiar ways.

When a child, he longed to clasp one,
The old folks cried, "Don't,
You are much too young." And he obeyed.

Later, as a boy, they said,
"The bought ones carry germs.
To touch might bring a bad disease
And ruin you for life. In any case,
a god is watching, quick to pounce,
should you touch forbidden fruit."

At last they let him have one tree
whose fruit was his alone to taste,
provided that he took to nourish it
and take his bites at proper intervals
and in approved ways.

And this he did quite faithfully,
although at times his taste buds hungered
for more exotic fruit.
In his old age, the customs changed
and fruit restrictions disappeared.

By that time his teeth were gone.
He could not bite an apple were he paid.

Now with others like himself
he sits inside a cinema
watching apple-eating free-for-alls.

The classic examples of children's poets getting rid of triteness by misapplication and hence creating novelty occur in the poetry of Edward Lear and Lewis Carroll. Lear's best known is probably "The Owl and the Pussycat" but the finest example of life-giving, not of triteness in any poem occurs in Lewis Carroll's "Jabberwocky". It is the finest justification of such a cold-blooded technique that I know in all poetry and encourages us to believe, for a time, anything is possible.

---

48 Fred Cogswell *Pearls*, Ragweed Press, Charlottetown, 1983.

The Nature and Function
of Poetry

Text of a talk given to the League of Canadian Poets in June, 1984.

In a very real sense, it is impossible to state what poetry is or what its functions may be. When Jesus Christ stood before Pilate and the Roman governor asked him, *What is truth?* the Word-made-Flesh had only silence for reply, for he knew that, as Shelley's Demogorgon was to say later, "The deep truth is imageless". In this sense, then, poetry *is*. Words about poetry are only words. It is easier, therefore, to state what poetry is not rather than what it is.

Just as it is impossible to state in any ultimate way what poetry is or what poetry is for, it is also impossible for the poet writing a poem to express his vision of experiential reality which prompted its creation in the first place. There is a gap between whatever reality our senses and memory apprehend—the experiential world—and the effect we produce through words that try either to correspond or to respond to it. As T.S. Eliot puts it in "The Hollow Men,"

"Between the idea
And the reality
Between the motion
And the act
Falls the Shadow"

and

"Between the conception
And the creation
Between the emotion
And the response
Falls the Shadow."

Yet the principal function of poetry through the ages seems to have been to close the gap between two realities —the reality of experience and the reality of words.

This is an impossible feat from the point of view of scientific accuracy—partly because of the complex nature of the words we use to express and communicate experience, and partly because of our readers' subjective responses to them. Words have a birth, growth, change, life, and death of their own, and individual circumstances in every human being's life give different nuances in meaning and feeling assigned to them.

The relation between symbol and object has varied with the development of society. In simpler, more primitive societies, there was a closer, more kinetic relationship between symbol and object, "the word was identical to the thing." Under such circumstances, poetry flourished easily, and the two worlds, the experiential and the symbolic, came closer to becoming one world than at any other time in history. Conversely, in a sophisticated, complex society with varying life-styles and degrees of specialism in occupation and education, the task of a poet in expressing experience for the sake of perpetuating it with any degree of accuracy in the minds and hearts of readers becomes hopeless and absurd and the social function of poetry tends to fall into disrepute. This can be seen, for example, in Greek literature. The myths, the epics of Homer, even the epigrams of Simonides—these were public poems written and appreciated by a whole culture, but in the Alexandrian period of Greek development, poets wrote only for themselves and small coteries whose taste and education were like their own.

A second difficulty in making the symbolic universe an expression of the experiental universe lies in the temporal dimension. My own poem, "Art," expresses this dilemma succinctly:

> Light bird of life
> Your death is sealed
> Even as we glimpse
> The form revealed:
>
> Strong though you soar,
> Marble, notes, words
> Kill the brave flight
> With static swords.

The experiential universe is one in which a multiplicity of things occur and are experienced simultaneously by a sentient organism, whereas in the symbolic universe—until recently at least—the nature of syntactical language is such that events were described, actions detailed, and backgrounds supplied serially. Apart from concrete poetry, most poetic devices are non-serial, although several threads may be carried on, imperfectly but almost simultaneously by our poetic devices. We can suggest colour or mood by careful placing of words and by using moods that have corresponding sounds, and by a combination of rhythm, type of sound, and emotional nuance in vocabulary, we can impart much more than a simple experience. At the same time, though, after we have written our "This is how the water comes down to Lodore," we have only to gaze at any real Niagara—or Lodore—to note the difference and despair.

An instrument can only function within its range, and words do not have the simultaneity, the vividness, nor the accuracy to render the equivalent of the most ordinary events. In this sense, realism and poetry are contradictory, and a poet who tries by eschewing metaphor and imagination and by "telling it like it is," simply, concretely, and without ornament, may succeed in imparting a limited kind of vision of reality, but he is not writing truth. To be imageless one's self does not necessarily convey the deep truth, even though that truth may be, as Shelley claims, "imageless."

If the nature and function of poetry is not, in our time, truth, what then is it? I maintain that modern poetry is a game like chess, baseball, or, better still, it is a one-person game like long-distance running where one competes essentially against one's self. Words are the counters one uses, readers and critics are one's audience, and the duration and shape of the game are determined by the interplay between the poet and certain rules that he or she has adopted for the duration of the game. The quality of the game can only be truly determined by those who know the rules.

The twentieth century is becoming more and more a century of games. Almost always now in life, events occur which are independent of our will, or against it. The myth of freedom, the myth of liberal democracy is becoming less and less tenable in an increasingly crowded, interrelated, and bureaucratic world. In a world of routine and mechanization, work becomes something that is often frustrating, something that is often endured rather than welcomed, and something to escape from. Mind was not meant to be subject to mindless machines and mindless processes. Therefore that part of us that longs for creative scope, for feeling, for imagination, finds itself increasingly turning elsewhere. One path is that of escape, a matter of losing one's identity by merging in a spectator sport or the sensational lives of soap-opera characters. This is to become a cipher, a complete victim of the pressures of current time and place. As our work becomes less fulfilling and meaningful, our play must become more so; otherwise we are doomed.

Our best hope right now, to survive as meaningful human beings, it seems to me, is to fulfil our creative impulses in hobbies and crafts. Within this play cycle, either as poet or reader of poetry we will find that poetry has much to offer. The name of the game that it involves is creation. A poet takes an experience, a group of experiences from the experiential world, and by recombining them in imagination and by taking advantage of the fact that symbols have a life of their own and shape themselves almost as though they were doing the writing themselves, he can create a new experience, an experience which, in turn, can engross others through their faculties of imagination and empathy. Although it will not be the experiential reality or realities that prompted its creation, it will be something new and unique in the universe that the words have somehow managed to create. Every poem is a universe, a coming together of ingredients in a new way, and I strongly suspect that every poet is more catalyst than god in the creative process. Often a good poem writes itself.

I do not intend to spend much time discussing the various forms, techniques, and subjects which are allowed in the game of poetry. In the totality of time, poets have written on every conceivable subject in every viable form and very often, with the passing of time the particular forms and the particular motives that inspired the poets' themes have lost their interest. Nevertheless, the poems still live. Who cares today, as Dante once cared, for the dispute between the rival factions of the Guelphs and the Ghibellines, yet *The Divine Comedy* which this rivalry inspired is still read with interest and imagination. The reason, I think, lies in a kind of timeless empathy that some poems have the faculty of creating. In Shakespeare's "Hamlet", the Danish prince, musing on the actor's genuine emotion while playing a role about the Trojan War, exclaims, "What's he to Hecuba that he should weep/For her?" This prompted me once to write a sonnet, elaborating Shakespeare's thought. It is called "Act of Love":

Although the space between us lies immense
There floats across the void from him to me
The finespun gossamer of poetry
Drawn from the entrails of experience.

Not like a web that catches flies by chance
And lets them wither to oblivion:
This is an act of love whose touch is one
With all of mind and muscle's nervous dance.

A Trojan plain, the sound of martial drums,
A withered crone, face torn by grief and fear
Among the press of Grecian victory.
No need to ask the question now: What's he
To Hecuba that he should weep for her?
I read, and in my tears the answer comes.

This brings me back, however, to the temporal dimension. Despite the universality of some poems and art forms, every age has its own peculiar rhythm or tempo, recognizable in such words as "classic," "baroque," or "rococo." A certain period becomes associated with, for example, the minuet; another with the waltz; still another with the fox-trot, and so on, down to, or up to, the jitterbug, depending on the point of view. To write as though one accepted the style of the age in which one's life had never occurred is, in a certain sense, not to have lived. In the seventeenth century lyrics by Donne and Herbert we enjoy the life we find in them because, although the attitudes and tempo which produced them are now dead, they were alive when they wrote them, and hence, by empathy, can come alive for us. But the religious lyrics of Francis Thompson, or even more those of A.J.M. Smith, that imitate the mannerisms of Donne and Herbert's day, despite their formal perfection, cannot come alive to us because they are self-conscious and were never in any unconscious sense alive to their authors. They were written from the outside in, not from the inside out. At the same time, Thompson's "Daisy" and Smith's "The Wisdom of Old Jelly Roll" are very meaningful because they come from the living experience of their authors. I know that it is unfashionable to praise didactic poetry, but strength of conviction can give incentive to artistic excellence, as Shaw well argues in "Man and Superman," and it is dangerous to condemn poetry on the ground that it is didactic. A list of didactic poets reads like an honour roll of poetry: Homer, Hesiod, Aristophanes, Sophocles, Virgil, Dante, Chaucer, Spenser, Shakespeare, Milton, Blake, Wordsworth, Goethe, Tennyson, Eliot, Yeats, to name a few.

At the same time, however, a writer who is dominated too much by the fashions of his own time—particularly a one-fashioned time—is in danger. He may never become what his full potential may be because he has settled too soon on something that suits him facilely and wins him quick praise. This is really what I have against the literary dictatorship of leading poets, professors, and critics. Very often, they succeed so well with styles and views of poetry that their immediate followers are content to follow their example without thinking that they themselves may only be minor poets. If had they tried other things, experimented more, and developed their own style, although they might not have succeeded at first, they might ultimately have both enlarged their own work, and the area of poetry itself. I am extremely happy with the current Canadian poetry scene because it has become one in which few can dictate how a poet should play the poetry game. As a result, we do have today a variety of form, theme, and sensibility such as has been found at no previous time in our literary history.

There are many pessimists, however, who say that this variety has been achieved at the expense of greatness. Where are the major Canadian poets in this *mélange*? It is always easier for poets to establish themselves, for the time being at least, as major poets in ages when the canons of poetry are relatively uniform. If all poets are trying to do the same things in the same way, it is relatively simple to determine how well comparatively each is succeeding. In an age of variety, however, when many people are attempting differing things in differing styles, the critic's task is much more difficult.

> And at the far end of the walk we would find these
>   apples
> On trees strayed almost to the edge of the forest,
> Reaching through the far away of that land
> For autumn epitomized in a single globe.

This movement, consisting mainly of poets united by family ties and a sense of place, mainly Fredericton, captured the imaginations of literate New Brunswickers for several generations. The poetic success of yet another

Fredericton poet from the same circle, Francis Sherman, only strengthened the tradition. When I grew up during the 1920s and 1930s, that tradition was my teachers' idea of what poetry ought to be, and it was my own idea as well. I think this was because our communities still possessed the innocent faith in the goodness of God and His universe-a faith that these poets, regardless of their personal lives or what they wrote in prose, were careful to incorporate, implicitly or explicitly, in their poetry. In New Brunswick, this view of life survived World War I and the boom and depression that followed it. In fact, in my community it lasted until World War II. Geographical isolation, freedom from massive population centres, freedom from industrialization, and the strength of evangelical Christianity favoured its retention. When I came back to Canada after World War II, was released from the Army, and enrolled as a freshman at the University of New Brunswick, I found that it had, apart from a few vestiges, disappeared. At the university, as elsewhere—wherever the mass-media had penetrated— innocence had seemingly given way to experience—faith in universal goodness hardly seemed possible any more.

Internal visions of the New Brunswick landscape were darker, harsher now. It seemed that a new poetry was required to express the narrowness, the limitations, the doubts and frustrations of human lives in New Brunswick. This would be a poetry that concentrated less on the physical aspects of nature and more on men, and women's lives; it would, in the fragmented society that now seemed to be, have a limited and not a universal appeal, and it ought to be an honest, direct response to personal experience or expression of personal vision rather than an attempt to establish further platitudes for an entire society.

As people grow and change, so do the games they play. As life-styles become freer and deviate more, so too should the arts and crafts that express individual needs and fulfil thwarted feelings and imaginations. As a matter of fact, the present has become freest in the arts because the participating arts have become almost the sole repository of freedom. Logistics—the very pressures and paces of urban living and population growth and the inter-relatedness of modern economic life—have so circumscribed the individual's freedom of action that he or she has turned more and more to fantasy and to violent spectator sports to escape these pressures. This turning to fantasy and to spectator sports is a negative response to the frustration of the human will. The "thinking reed" merely loses itself in its identification with the wills of others and forgets for a spell the wind that has bowed it down. Such a reed will never become more than a reed, who for a little while is allowed to become a voyeur of a freedom he does not truly possess. The sports-fantasies that take the place of the heaven that once served to keep the masses in their place when no one wanted change— these provide a shadowy, vicarious existence at best. Those who are wise today turn, not to fantasy or spectator sport, but rather to playing games themselves as participants, either directly in person, or symbolically in creating or reading literature. In imaginative creation alone, man can truly "shatter this sorry scheme of things to bits" and "remold it nearer to the heart's desire."

To what ought the poet to be true in this new symbolic universe-making?

I would suggest that in a world of conformist advertising and pressures toward conformity, a poet ought to express—primarily for his own satisfaction and understanding—his personal reaction to experience, reinforced by all the knowledge at his disposal and put into forms and contexts which he has, after extensive trial and error, found best suited to his individual powers of expression. If others publish his poetry, pay for him to read at universities, give him writing grants, he is lucky—and let him enjoy that luck. He should not kid himself, however, that he is any more creative nor fulfils himself more than does the poet who lacks the same good success in the external world. Both poets, by their writing, are fulfilling the creative urge which is part of all nature, but which, when expressed in its highest physical, mental, and spiritual form is the kind of impulse that drives men to start and complete poems. If the only person moved by the catalytic activity of the poem were the poet himself, I would still say that he is blessed in his creation, for he is a creator, one with all creators since God and Adam, present at the first great naming of things, and carrying on a purpose for which it would not be too egotistical to suppose the human race was created to fulfil. He has not merely taken meekly from life or ran away from it. He has added something new and uniquely his own to the total scheme of things.

Of all games that life has devised, the most meaningful—and the most bound up with pain and leisure is creation. Of all the forms of human creation, the most complex and the one which absorbs all the attributes of humanity is poetry. It is like the earth, though. To see it shine at its most beautiful, we must go to the moon. Almost always we are too close to it in the here and now. We are also too saturated in it. To see poetry the way Keats saw it, we must deprive ourselves of it and then come to it again after the need becomes a positive hunger. Only when we look at it then can we truly feel like the Keats who read Chapman's *Homer* or like

> Stout Cortez when with eagle eye
> He stared at the Pacific, and all his men
> Looked at each other with a wild surmise,
> Silent, upon a peak in Darien.

Since there is not apt to be a shortage of poems to read and since the individual poem, like the individual star in the Milky Way, is apt to become a bit blurred by the many others of its kind, poetry readers, I am afraid, are apt to have much less excitement from single poems in the future than they would have done in Chaucer's time. I would therefore recommend that they become poets instead. There is nothing like a new poem to look at—if it is your own creation and you have just finished it. That experience is more than worth all the agony of creation, and it is open to every one who wishes to have it. In this context, the greater the formal difficulty contained in the poem one has set out to do, the greater the joy to have overcome that difficulty. In this connection, note the sestina, "The Heart of Form," which I wrote:

Out of mystery what is set down here
Is born. Perhaps I chose the theme at work,
But know not how or why it came to me.
Nor can I say about the words I write
Whether they merely rise up to fit the form
Or whether form itself from content comes.

Were you to ask, I could not tell what comes
Foremost in lines that flow through eye and ear.
The final consonance of feeling, form
And thought you find here was not in this work
Or anywhere when I began to write
Save for one image that Yeats gave to me

From it associations came, by me
Chosen or discarded as the whole welcomes
Or rejects them. These led me to seek right
Words, sounds, rhythms, images that cohere,
And nothing halted the unfolding work
Until it fused in this way with the form.

Between amorphous thought and shaping form
Creation's tension lies, epitome
Of many diverse processes that work
To form the dance of life. When music comes
The dancers leap to time and tune, but here
Music's in the mind, limbs but words I write.

How know the dancer from the dance? The right
Answer could be that dance is ideal form
Though dancers differ, but when the two cohere

The dancer makes the dance. It seems to me
No dance is meaningful unless it comes
From the dancer's best, still and strength at work.

A poet-dancer's human, Though at work
In one mind, a quicksilver god may write
With words well shaped to fit a dream of form,
I may not know his presence when he comes
Or, if I do, may still put off from me
The power in him that jars with now and here.

Here, reader, is a sample of the work
That comes to me. Judge now how much I write
Is owed to mystery, how much to form.

Having brought this discourse to a climactic ending, I
suddenly feel that perhaps I have not made a sufficient
distinction between what I call a poem and what I call a
non-poem which resembles it very closely. There is, in
fact, no formal difference between the two.

The difference lies really in the attitude of the poet-
creator to the universe. The non-poem is the product of
what Aldous Huxley calls "emotional engineering." In it
the poet takes into account the prejudices, connotations,
predilections of his readers, and manipulates them for
effect according to formulas that can be learned at almost
any creative writing course. As a result, the reader is given
an illusory experience that parallels his own without
enlarging it. The non-poem preaches only to the con-
verted. In this connection, I cannot help but think of
Ogden Nash, who will not flog a horse, in his words,

until he knows indubitably that it has been dead so long that no one could conceivably object to his poem's actions.

The true poem, as opposed to the non-poem, offers its readers an alternate universe to that in which they normally dwell. If it is sufficiently well done, it will offer a universe that coheres sufficiently for them to accept it imaginatively even though their own innate prejudices might have normally led them to reject it. As a result of meeting alternate universes in this way, readers can come to realize the wonder, the variety, and the possibilities of life. Hence, the trap of circumstances in which they find themselves may become at the same time both more galling and less inevitable.

As William Blake wrote, "We become what we behold."

Therefore if we behold only machines and stereotypes, we tend to become only machines and stereotypes and to atrophy within those areas of our minds that exist to make us more. If we read true poems, however, and hence obtain multiple visions of reality we are generated into feelings, actions, and imaginative ventures that are bound to make us—and the society of which we are members—more than we would otherwise have become. If poetry needs any social justification—apart from what it gives personally to its practitioners—this is it.

June, 1984

A Selected Bibliography of Fred's Work

Compiled by Kathleen Forsythe and Wendy Scott
As Cogswell's first published poem appeared in 1939, and he is still an active writer of poems and translations, this bibliography can only be a partial reflection of a multi-faceted career spanning sixty-five years. The titles below are arranged chronologically and divided by format.

Collected Poems (Books and Pamphlets)

The Stunted Strong. Fredericton: University of New Brunswick, 1954. (Fiddlehead Poetry Books; no. 1). 16 p.

The Haloed Tree. Toronto: Ryerson Press, c1956. (Ryerson Poetry Chap-Book 164) 16 p.

Descent from Eden. Toronto: Ryerson Press, 1959. 38 p.

Lost Dimension. Dulwich Village [England]: College Press, Outpost Publications, 1960. 12 p.

Star People. Fredericton: Fiddlehead Poetry Books, 1968. [48 p.]

Immortal Plowman. Fredericton: Fiddlehead Poetry Books, 1969. 38 p.

In Praise of Chastity. Fredericton: University of New Brunswick, 1970. (The New Brunswick Chapbooks; No. 12.) 1 v.

The Chains of Liliput. Fredericton, N.B.: Fiddlehead Poetry Books, 1971. 32 p. ISBN: 0-919196-00-4.

The House Without a Door. Fredericton, N.B.:
Fiddlehead Poetry Books, 1973. 32 p. ISBN:
0-9191975-4X

Light Bird of Life: Selected Poems. Fredericton, N.B:
Fiddlehead Poetry Books, 1974. 62 p. ISBN:
0-9191977-79.

Against Perspective. Fredericton: Fiddlehead Poetry
Books, 1977. 47 p.

*A Long Apprenticeship: The Collected Poems of Fred
Cogswell.* Fredericton: Fiddlehead Poetry Books,
1980. 225 p. (Fiddlehead Poetry Books series no.
302.) ISBN 0-864920-00-8.
Re-issued 1983 with cover photography by Reg
Balch. (Fiddlehead Poetry Book No. 303.)

Our Stubborn Strength. [Toronto]: League of Canadian
Poets, [1980]. [8] p.

Pearls: Poems by Fred Cogswell. Charlottetown, P.E.I.:
Ragweed Press, 1983. 62 p. ISBN 0-920304-21-4.

Fred Cogswell: Selected Poems. Edited by Antonio
D'Alfonso. Montreal: Guernica Editions, 1983.
59 p. ISBN 0-919349-22-6 (bound edition);
0-919349-21-8 (pbk).
"The poems in this selection were all taken, except
for "Fireflies: Cape Traverse", from *A Long
Apprenticeship"* (Preface, p. 7).

Meditations: 50 Sestinas. Charlottetown: Ragweed Press,
1983. 56 p. ISBN 0-920304-48-6.

An Edge to Life. Saint John, N.B.: Purple Wednesday
Society, 1987. (No. 1 of a series entitled Seven
Times Five.) [7] p. ISBN: 0-920492-08-8.

The Best Notes Merge. Ottawa: Borealis Press, 1988. 59
p, ISBN 0-88887-899-0 (bound); 0-88887-901-6
(pbk.)

Black and White Tapestry. Ottawa: Borealis Press, 1989.
79 p. ISBN 0-88887-915-6 (bound); 0-88887-
917-2 (pbk.)

Watching an Eagle. Ottawa: Borealis Press, 1991. 73 p.

In Praise of Old Music. Ottawa: Borealis Press, 1992.
75 p. ISBN 0-88887-134-1 (bound); 0-88887-136-8
(pbk.).

When the Right Light Shines. Ottawa: Borealis Press,
1992. 74 p. ISBN 0-88887-122-8- (bound); 0-
88887-124-4 (pbk.)

In My Own Growing. Ottawa: Borealis Press, 1993. 77 p.
ISBN 0-88887-113-9 (bound); 0-88887-115-5
(pbk.).

As I See It. Ottawa, Canada: Borealis Press, 1994. 74 p.
ISBN 0-88887-148-1 (bound); 0-88887-150-3
(pbk.)

The Trouble With Light. Nepean [Ontario], Canada:
Borealis Press, 1996. 84 p. ISBN 0-88887-919-9
(bound); 0-88887-140-6 (pbk.)

Folds. Nepean, [Ontario] Canada: Borealis Press, 1997.
90 p. ISBN 0-88887-169-4 (bound); 0-88887-171-
6 (pbk.).

A Double Question . . . Nepean, Canada: Borealis Press,
1999. 88 p. ISBN 0-88887-838-9 (bound); 0-
88887-840-0 (pbk.).

With Vision Added. Nepean, Canada: Borealis Press,
2000. 109 p. ISBN 0-88887-847-8 (bound);
0-88887-845-1 (pbk.).

Deeper Than Mind. Ottawa: Borealis Press Ltd., 2001.
114 p. ISBN 0-88887-263-1.

Dried Flowers. Ottawa: Borealis Press, 2002. vii, 108 p.
ISBN 0-88887-208-9.

Ghosts. Ottawa: Borealis, 2002. vii, 107 p. ISBN 0-
88887-216-X.

Later in Chicago. Ottawa: Borealis Press, 2003. 110 p.
ISBN 0-88887-212-7.

The Kindness of Stars. Ottawa, Borealis Press, 2004. ix,
126 p. ISBN 0-88887-205-4.

Poetry in Translation

Henryson, Robert. *The Testament of Cresseid.* [from the
Scottish]. Toronto: Ryerson, c1957. 24 p. (Ryerson
Poetry Chap Books; 168.) 1957.

"Beowulf." Translated by F.W. Cogswell and A.M.
Kinloch. In *Our Literary Heritage.* Ed., Desmond
Pacey. Toronto: Ryerson Press and Macmillan
Company of Canada, 1967, pp. 4-39. [Cogswell's
rendering into poetry from Kinloch's prose transla-
tion, respecting the metre and verse forms of the
original. Also in 2nd edition revised by Michael
Pacey (McGraw-Hill, 1982).

One Hundred Poems of Modern Quebec. Translated by
Fred Cogswell. Fredericton: Fiddlehead Press, 1970.
91 pp.

A Second Hundred Poems of Modern Quebec. Edited
and translated by Fred Cogswell. Fredericton:
Fiddlehead Poetry Books, 1971. 80 p. ISBN
919196-57-8.

Lapointe, Gatien. *Confrontation = Face à face.*
Fredericton: Fiddlehead Poetry Books, 1973. 26 p.:
ISBN: 0-919197-64-7

The Poetry of Modern Quebec: An Anthology. Edited and
translated by Fred Cogswell. Montreal: Harvest
House, 1976. 206 p. (The French Writers of
Canada series.) ISBN 88772-1680 (bound); 88772-
2253 (pbk.).

Nelligan, Emile. *The Complete Poems of Emile Nelligan.*
Edited, translated, and with an introduction by
Fred Cogswell. Montreal: Harvest House, 1983.
(The French Writers of Canada series.) xxiv, 120 p.

Lasnier, Rina: "The Body of Christ", "At the Water's
Edge", "The Deaf"; Hébert, Anne: "Castle-Life",
"There is Some One, To Be Sure", "Eve"; Cloutier,
Cécile: "By Way of Error", "If Only my Body", "A
Leaf", "Against My Country", "I Took", "I Would
Like to Be True" [Translations from the French]. In
*Longman Anthology of World Literature By Women:
1875-1975.* Marian Arkin and Barbara Shollar.
New York: Longman, c1989. ISBN 0-582285-59-3.

Unfinished Dreams: Contemporary Poetry of Acadie. Fred
Cogswell & Jo-Anne Elder, Translators and Editors.
With an Introduction by Raoul Boudreau.
Fredericton: Goose Lane Editions, 1990. xiii, xxvii,
172 p. ISBN 0-86492-132-2.

Published in French as: *Rêves inachevés : anthologie de
poésie acadienne contemporaine.* Sous la direction de
Fred Cogswell et Jo-Ann Elder; avec une introduc-
tion de Raoul Boudreau. Moncton, N.-B. : Éditions
d'Acadie, 1990. 212 p. ISBN 2-76000-179-2.

Chiasson, Herménégilde. *Climates.* Translated by Fred
    Cogswell and Jo-Anne Elder. Fredericton: Goose
    Lane Editions, 1999. 119 p. ISBN 0-86492-274-4.
Chiasson, Herménégilde. *Conversations.* Translated by
    Jo-Anne Elder and Fred Cogswell. Fredericton: Goose
    Lane Editions, c2001. 1 v. ISBN 0-86492-319-8.

Literary History and Criticism
"Moses Hardy Nickerson: a Study." *Dalhousie Review,* v.
    38 (winter 1959), pp. 472-485.
"Nineteenth Century Poetry in the Maritimes and
    Problems of Research." *Newsletter of the
    Bibliographical Society of Canada,* vol. 5 (September
    1961), pp. 5-19.
"E.J. Pratt's Literary Reputation." *Canadian Literature,*
    no. 19 (winter 1964), pp. 6-12.
"Newfoundland (1715-1880). In: *Literary History of
    Canada.* Eds. C.F. Klinck et al. Toronto: University
    of Toronto Press, 1965. 2nd ed., 1976. pp. 68-71.
"The Maritime Provinces (1720-1815), Ibid, pp. 71-82.
"Haliburton". Ibid. pp 92-101.
"Literary Activity in the Maritime Provinces (1815-
    1880)", Ibid, pp. 102-124.
"From the Canadian Private Presses." [Poetry
    Chapbooks.] *Fiddlehead,* no. 68 (Spring 1966),
    pp. 68-80.
"Eros and Literature." *Mosaic,* v. 1, no. 2 (January
    1968), pp. 103-111.
"Until Time Ends Bad Art: Maritime Writers Must
    Preserve." *The Globe and Mail* (Toronto), Jan. 14,
    1968.

"The Poetry of Modern Quebec." In *On Canada: Essays in Honour of Frank H. Underhill.* Ed. by Norman Penlington. [Toronto]: University of Toronto Press, [c1971]. pp. 54-70. ISBN: 0-802017-25-8.

"Early, May Agnes (Fleming)". *Dictionary of Canadian Biography,* volume 10 (1871-1880). Toronto: University of Toronto Press, 1972, pp. 268-269.

"The French Canadian Novel and the Problem of Social Change." *Journal of Canadian Fiction,* v. 1, no. 2 (spring 1972), pp. 65-68.

"Birney (Alfred Earle 1904-)." *Contemporary Literary Criticism,* Vol. 1. Ed., Carolyn Riley. Detroit: Gale Research Company, 1973. p. 34.

"Haliburton, Thomas Chandler." *Dictionary of Canadian Biography,* v. 9 (1861-1870), pp. 348-357. Toronto: University of Toronto Press, 1976.

"Literary Traditions in New Brunswick." *Transactions of the Royal Society of Canada. Series IV,* v. 15 (1977), pp. 287-299.

"Little Magazines and Small Presses in Canada." in *Figures in a Ground: Canadian Essays on Modern Literature Collected in Honor of Sheila Watson.* Ed. by D. Bessai and D. Jackel. Saskatoon: Western Producer Prairie Books, 1978. pp. 162-173.

"Symbol and Decoration: 'The Pipes of Arill.'" In: *The Duncan Campbell Scott Symposium, Université d'Ottawa/University of Ottawa, 1979.* Ed. and with an introduction by K.P. Stich. Ottawa: University of Ottawa Press, 1980. (Re-Appraisals, Canadian Writers series.) ISBN 2-760343-86-3. pp. 47-54.

"Charles G.D. Roberts." In: *Canadian Writers and Their Works: Essays on Form, Context, and Development: Volume 2: Poetry.* Ed. by Robert Lecker, Jack David, Ellen Quigley. Introduced by George Woodcock. [Toronto]: ECW Press, 1983. pp. 187-232.

Charles G.D. Roberts and His Works. Downsview, Ont.: ECW Press, 1983.

"The Classical Poetry of Sir Charles G.D. Roberts"; "The Achievement of Sir Charles G.D. Roberts: An Assessment Panel." *The Sir Charles G.D, Roberts Symposium, 1983.* Edited and with an introduction by Glenn Clever. [Ottawa] : University of Ottawa Press, 1984, c1983. (Reappraisals, Canadian Writers series.) ISBN: 0-776643-90-8

Roberts, Charles G.D. *Collected Poems of Sir Charles G.D. Roberts: A Critical Edition.* Ed. by Desmond Pacey; assistant editor, Graham Adams. Wolfville, N.S.: Wombat Press, c1985. [Introduction by Fred Cogswell.] ISBN 0-969082-23-5. pp.

Miller, Muriel. *Bliss Carman: Quest and Revolt.* St. John's, Nfld.: Jesperson Press, 1985. [Introduction by Fred Cogswell.] ISBN 0-920502-62-8.

The Bicentennial Lectures on New Brunswick Literature. Malcolm Ross, Fred Cogswell, Marguerite Maillet. Sackville, N.B.: Centre for Canadian Studies, Mount Allison University, c1985. 62 pp. ISBN 0-888280-45-9.

"Alden Nowlan as Regional Atavist." In *Encounters and Explorations: Canadian Writers and European Critics.* Eds., Franz K. Stanzel and Waldemar Zacharasiewicz. Wurzburg: Konigshausen &

Neumann, 1986. pp. 37-55.
Reprinted with minor revisions from *Studies in Canadian Literature*, vol. 11, no. 2 (Fall 1986), pp. 206-225.

Charles Mair. Toronto : ECW Press, 1988. ISBN 0-920763-70-7. Unpaged monograph, reprinted from "Charles Mair." In *Canadian Writers and Their Works. Poetry Series*, Volume 1. Ed. by Robert Lecker, Jack David, Ellen Quigley. Toronto: ECW Press, 1988. ISBN 0-920802-43-5 (set); v.1: 0-920763-69-3. pp. 119-155.

"English Poetry in New Brunswick before 1880." In *A Literary and Linguistic History of New Brunswick*. Editor, Reavely Gair. Fredericton: Goose Lane Editions, 1985. pp.

"English Prose Writing in New Brunswick." Ibid, pp.

Roberts, Charles G. D. Introduction [to] *The Collected Letters of Sir Charles G.D., Roberts*, Laurel Boone, Editor. Fredericton: Goose Lane Editions, c1989. ISBN: 0-864920-94-6.

"Challenge and Response in Quebec Poetry: The Existentialist Movement." in *A Celebration of Canada's Arts, 1930-1970*. Ed. by Glen Carruthers and Gordana Lazarevich. Toronto: Canadian Scholars Press, 1996. xxi, 244 p. ISBN: 1-551300-64-8.

"The Poetry of Revolution in Modern Quebec" *Lakehead University Review*, Vol. VII, Number 2, Vol. VIII, Numbers 1 and 2.

Festschrift

Scroll. Ed. by Greg Cook. Wolfville, N.S.: Wombat
    Press, c1980. (Wombat Literary Series, no. 1.)
    1 portfolio (51 sheets).
    [Collection of works by various authors, presented
    to Fred Cogswell on his retirement as publisher of
    Fiddlehead Poetry Books.]

Theses

The Canadian Novel from Confederation Until World
    War One. Thesis: (M.A.) University of New
    Brunswick. Microfilm of typescript. Fredericton,
    N.B.: University of New Brunswick, 1950. 1 reel;
    35 mm.
The Concept of America in English Romantic
    Literature. Ph.D., University of Edinburgh, 1952.
    p. 308.

Publications Edited by Cogswell

A Canadian Anthology: Poems from The Fiddlehead,
    1945-1959. Fredericton: The Fiddlehead, no. 50,
    (Fall 1961).
Scott, Sir Walter. *Ivanhoe.* Editor, Fred Cogswell, New
    York: Airmont Publishing Co, 1964.
The Arts in New Brunswick. [Centennial Edition.] Ed.
    by R.A. Tweedie, W. Stewart MacNutt.
    [Fredericton]: Brunswick Press, c1967. pp. 280.
The Enchanted Land: Canadian Poetry for Young Readers.
    Compiled by Thelma Reid Lower and Frederick
    William Cogswell. Toronto: W.J. Gage, 1967. pp. 150.

The Atlantic Anthology. Edited by Fred Cogswell.
Charlottetown: Ragweed Press, 1984. 2 volumes.
Volume I, Prose. ISBN: 0-920304-23-0; volume 2,
Poetry. ISBN 0-920304-30-3.

One Hundred Poems of Modern Quebec. Op. cit., 1970.

A Second Hundred Poems of Modern Quebec. Op. cit.,
1971.

Five New Brunswick Poets: Elizabeth Brewster, Fred
Cogswell, Robert Gibbs, Alden Nowlan, Kay Smith.
Fredericton: The Fiddlehead, Dept. of English,
University of New Brunswick, [1962]. (A Fiddlehead
book.) pp. 64.

The Poetry of Modern Quebec: An Anthology. Edited and
translated by Fred Cogswell. Op. cit., 1976.

Mysterious Special Sauce. Judged and selected by Fred
Cogswell, Kay Smith, Constance Soulikas [i.e.,
Soulikias]; [Bill Warden, Ed.] [Toronto]: Pandora
Charitable Trust, Canadian Council of Teachers of
English, [1982 printing].
[Cover title: Pandora Poems by Canadian Students]
129 p.

Biographical Articles Canadian Writers, Ed. W, E,
New, Gale Research Company, Detroit:
By Fred Cogswell
Alden Nowlan (1933-1983)
Desmond Pacey (1917-1975)
Elizabeth Brewster (1922-)

Fred Cogswell:

As noted above, this selected bibliography does not represent the full range of Cogswell's literary output. His activities have included writing and translation, literary criticism and history, editor and publisher In addition to the works listed above, his poems and translations have appeared in Canadian and international magazines, literary journals, and multi-author collections; he has written book reviews for newspapers and journals; given papers at innumerable conferences, readings, and workshops; and, between 1954 and 1981, he was the editor and publisher of 307 titles in The Fiddlehead Poetry Books series. Recently, he and his daughter Kathleen Forsythe published two titles under the Cogswell Books imprint. His editing work also includes several years as editor of the literary journal *The Fiddlehead* (1952-1967), and of *The Humanities Association Bulletin.*

For his poetry, his work in promoting Canadian poetry and literature, and especially for his support and encouragement of emerging writers, Cogswell has received many awards, including the Bliss Carman Award for Poetry (1945 and 1947) and the Gold Medal from the Philippines Republic for Distinguished Poet and Magazine Editor (1957). In 1995 the Government of New Brunswick awarded him the Alden Nowlan Award for Excellence in Literary Arts. Other awards include The Order of Canada (1981), the Medal for the 125th Anniversary of Canada (1997), and the Queen's Golden Jubilee Medal (2002).

He is an honorary life member of the League of Canadian Poets, The Association of Canadian Publishers, The Atlantic Publishers Association, the New Brunswick Writers Association, and the Writers' Federation of New Brunswick. He is also on the Editorial Boards of *Studies in Canadian Literature* and of *Ellipse,* the journal of Canadian writing in translation. He holds honorary degrees from Saint Francis Xavier University (LLD, 1983); King's College (DCL, 1985), and Mount Allison University (LLD, 1988).

Wendy Scott
Montreal

Kathleen Forsythe
Vancouver

MEMBRE DE SCABRINI MEDIA

Québec, Canada
2004